make Love Everyday

12 Sure-fire ways to Celebrate your Marriage

JAY and LAURA LAFFOON

PRESS

ACW Press
Phoenix, Arizona 85013

Make Love Everyday: 12 Sure-Fire Ways to Celebrate Your Marriage
Copyright © 2002 Jay and Laura Laffoon
All rights reserved

Cover Design by Alpha Advertising
Front Cover Photo by Dan Wheeler, Wheeler Portrait Studio (989) 875-3869
Interior design by Pine Hill Graphics

Published by Celebrate Press

Packaged by ACW Press
5501 N. 7th Ave., #502
Phoenix, Arizona 85013
www.acwpress.com
The views expressed or implied in this work do not necessarily reflect those of ACW Press. Ultimate design, content, and editorial accuracy of this work is the responsibility of the author(s).

Library of Congress Cataloging-in-Publication Data

Laffoon, Jay.
    Make love everyday : 12 sure-fire ways to celebrate
your marriage! / Jay and Laura Laffoon. -- 1st ed.
    p. cm.
    ISBN: 1-892525-78-X

    1. Marriage. 2. Marriage--Religious aspects--
Christianity. I. Laffoon, Laura. II. Title.

HQ734.L34 2002   306.81
                         QBI02-200223

This book is dedicated to:

Jim, Doyce, Jayne, and Charlie

who taught us that marriage is a party!

Contents

Acknowledgments

Jay and Laura would like to say thanks to: Our kids for giving us two more reasons to celebrate every day. Our families who have stood behind us pushing us to follow the dreams the Lord put in our hearts. "Auntie Di" we could not do it without you! Debi, your words are a blessing from above! Our Core Team who make our conferences more like play than work. The "Gang" in Alma, you all know who you are…why live anywhere else! Ken and Diane Davis for believing. Danny and Betsy deArmas for everything! Marci Barton (Bill too) for fitting so perfectly into our crazy life. Finally, Jesus, the author and perfecter of our faith, who gives us the ultimate reason to celebrate!

A Note to Readers

We believe every marriage is a book just waiting to be written. Woven within the context of daily life is the tapestry of truth we all seek. Our marriage is unique and yet similar to every other marriage. We are very normal people with very normal lives who happen to believe that God intended marriage to be *celebrated!*

Our story unfolds in the pages of this book, along with some truths we have discovered. As you read, we trust you will be able to add some truth to the pages of the storybook which is unfolding in your marriage.

Most of the stories are written from Jay's perspective, as he is the storyteller in our family. The italicized portion is written from Laura's viewpoint. All of the content is a synthesis of our life together. We have found that the two of us have many differing views; however, the writing of this book has helped us realize the importance of life together and perfectly illustrates one of Laura's favorite comments: *"If we were both the same, one of us wouldn't be necessary."* Come, **celebrate** with us.

Introduction

July 3

O
n July 3, 1984, I moved from my hometown of Petoskey, Michigan to Atlanta, Georgia to begin a job I secured after graduating from college. On July 4, through mutual friends Chaz and Deaver Corzine, I was set up on a blind date with Laura Elizabeth Bass.

We arrived at Laura's house 30 minutes early. At this point, I became keenly aware of the first rule of blind dating, in fact, the first rule of any sort of dating: Don't show up half an hour early. I knocked on the door for what seemed like an eternity. After each knock, I turned to Chaz and Deaver and asked in disbelief, "Is this girl standing me up or what?" My self-esteem was withering by the millisecond.

We were just about to leave when the door sprang open. I don't fully remember my initial facial reaction, but I know I was surprised. Standing before me was a young woman wearing nothing but a T-shirt and boxer shorts. She had obviously just gotten out of the shower. Her hair was soaking wet and strung all over her face. She clutched a towel to her chest in an obvious attempt at modesty.

I stuck out my hand, and with every bit of personality I could muster I said, "Hi, I 'm Jay." Laura laughed with a girlish junior high giggle that said, "Glad to meet you, but I'm really embarrassed." She turned toward Deaver with a look that sent shivers down my spine. Come to think of it, I've seen that look a time or two...thousand times.

Chaz and I sat down in the living room and turned on the television, to watch "The Andy Griffith Show." Deaver accompanied

Laura while she readied herself. Twenty minutes later I learned the second rule of dating. When women go away together, miracles happen. I'm not sure of the how or why or the actual process of miracle making, but when it does, we men have absolutely no clue!

When Laura finally emerged from the hallway, I looked up and saw absolute beauty. The shower-soaked woman I met at the door had been transformed. All the basic parts were the same, but what materialized before my eyes was nothing short of miraculous. I saw pure, whole, genuine beauty. I now know why women go to the bathroom in groups. It's where they plan their next miracle.

The big date was to an Atlanta Braves baseball game. The game was okay. These were the 1984 Braves…perennial cellar dwellers. Now I'm a sports fan, but baseball reminds me of a chess game. Forty-five seconds of great excitement and entertainment, interrupted by 3-1/2 hours of boredom. I vaguely remember they played the Montreal Expos and I think the Braves won. I also vividly remember that the tickets cost too much, the food was awful, and Laura and I talked about everything.

I had been on dates with many members of the opposite sex. In fact, some of my best friends are females, but this was different. The conversation flowed like a mighty river, with a current that ran deep and strong. I was amazed by the intensity of our communication so early in the relationship.

After the game ended, the stadium instantly went dark and the Fourth of July fireworks display received its usual array of ooohs and ahhhs. Upon the grand finale, the lights illuminated, glowing dimly at first, then growing brighter and brighter.

Chaz, wanting to beat the crowd, grabbed Deaver's hand and bolted for the gate. She instinctively grabbed Laura's hand, and in turn, Laura grabbed mine. My heart leaped out of my chest. It was very strange. I've held girls' hands before and felt like my entire body would go into a seizure with arms, legs, and head reeling in every direction because of the ecstasy. This time, however, my heart was the only thing that jumped. It scared me to death.

The entire trip home I quietly analyzed the situation. Laura got out of the car so quick, with not so much as a goodnight handshake.

I mean, we held hands for crying out loud. I really wanted a kiss.

(Later I learned that the next morning over a bowl of cereal, Laura's mom asked how the date went. Without hesitation Laura replied, "Mom, I'm going to marry that man!")

Over the next ten days, I learned the third and final rule of dating: If a woman wants you, give up! They should teach a course in every college and university in America for men only entitled, "Give up 101." It would save a tremendous amount of pain and suffering on the part of men trying to flee the laser-guided tractor beam of a woman in love. If she wants you, you're caught. Dead meat. Game over!

The reason it doesn't work for men is that we have to change too much. Besides, men know what men want, and women know what men want. Men want women! It is said that the problem in relationships is that women don't know what they want. Laura will quickly correct me and say that women do know what they want. They want it all!

In a city of two million people, Laura (and to this day I still don't know how) managed to have our paths cross eight of the next ten days. The coup d'etats took place when she invited me to accompany her on a weekend trip to the mountains with friends. Saturday night, ten days after our blind date, in a log cabin on a mountain in North Carolina, I asked Laura Elizabeth Bass to be my wife. She coyly replied, "What took you so long?" The celebration began.

Prologue

The Ring

*T*hree hundred dollars! That was all the money I had in the world. After moving to Atlanta and paying my first month's rent, I had $300 left over. Laura knew I couldn't afford a ring, but she said "Yes" anyway. Sunday was a day sent straight from heaven. Carolina Blue sky, billowing clouds, and the drive back to Atlanta were all perfect. I lay in bed Sunday night, my heart on fire. I was in love, and nothing else in the world mattered. That is…until Monday morning.

As soon as I arrived at work, I sensed something was different. I'd only been there a week and a half, but something big was going down. The company for which I had moved to Atlanta, the reason I moved 1,000 miles from home, was closing its doors. I was out of work.

A worrier by nature, I like to have my "ducks in a row." Now, my life was upside down and inside out. No job. No money. No place to live. And a fiancée with no ring on her finger. As Dickens so aptly put it, "It was the best of times, it was the worst of times."

What would I tell Laura? What would I tell my parents? They hadn't been too sure about the security of this job in the first place.

Laura showed me a great deal about faith. "First," she said with a smile, "I have money. Second, you can live with my mom if you need to, and the ring…well, I'll get it when I get it. Now kiss me!" What a woman! At that moment I knew why I had moved to Atlanta and why I was here. It was to begin the rest of my life with the woman my mom had been praying for since I was young. I truly experienced peace in the midst of the storm.

When I called home to share the news, my mom immediately interrupted. "I'm so glad you called. I've got some business to cover with you." Without hesitation, she proceeded to tell me of a life insurance policy they had taken out on me years before. She told me I could keep it or cash it in. Hmmm, I thought, cash! I wasn't sure why we hadn't covered this "business" before I left home, but the thought of $2,000 in my grubby little palm was great news.

"Mom," I said, "Put dad on the other phone. I've got some good news and some bad news."

First I told them about Laura. "JAY WILLIAM LAFFOON, YOU DO NOT TELL YOUR MOTHER YOU'RE ENGAGED OVER THE PHONE AFTER KNOWING THIS GIRL ONLY TEN DAYS. I certainly hope this is the bad news."

"Well, Mom, actually that was the good news." Silence. Dead air. Nothing.

When you're on the phone there is nothing worse, nothing more painful than silence. "We trust you, son." Dad's voice was like a bell ringing from the steeple of a church—comforting and encouraging.

As we talked, it made sense as to why the insurance issue was now being discussed. I don't believe in coincidence. God's timing is perfect!

I could scrape by on $2,000 for quite some time, but I was a man on a mission. That money was my ticket to an engagement ring, and nothing would stand in my way.

After a bit of shopping, I picked up the ring. It was actually quite easy as Laura worked all day, giving me plenty of time. Her job as a summer counselor at a day camp was over August 1st, so we decided to go to Colorado to work at a camp my dad directed every summer. I devised a plan to give Laura the engagement ring on top of a mountain in the camp. It's called Soldiers Mountain, and lies on the backside of the range from the U.S. Air Force Academy. On top of the mountain is a cross fabricated from two pine trees and wedged between two large rocks. The view of Pikes Peak, and the surrounding mountain ranges from the summit of Soldier's Mountain, is nothing short of spectacular. I would give Laura the ring on top of Soldiers Mountain, at the foot of the cross.

We drove 20 hours straight from Atlanta to Colorado Springs, except for an hour in a rest area in western Kansas. The sunrise woke us and we were on our way, my little Toyota performing flawlessly.

Quaker Ridge Camp in Woodland Park, Colorado, at that time was managed by Harold and Carrie Masten, along with their son Marty. It's a rustic camp with a great feel, a super place for flat-landers to come to experience the mountains.

For the last month, Laura and I had been frequenting Pizza Hut for lunch. At the time they were running a "five minutes or it's free" deal. We would sit in the parking lot and wait for a large group to walk in, then we'd go in and say, "five minutes or free," and invariably we'd end up getting a free meal.

I had hidden the engagement ring and a bottle of champagne (given to me at the diamond store) in Laura's backpack. My idea was to get two pan pizzas (actually pay for them) and hike to the top of the mountain for a picnic, then give her the ring.

Quaker Ridge is a good 20-minute drive from Woodland Park. Up Highway 67 toward Deckers, turning off at the "Meadows" sign in the Pikes Peak National Forest. Travel two miles up the winding cutbacks of the dirt drive, and suddenly you arrive in a whole new world—a refuge, isolated from life's hustle and bustle.

The hike up Soldiers Mountain also takes about 20 minutes, depending on your physical condition and the number of times you stop to take picture after picture of this place touched by the hand of God. I kept prodding Laura to get to the top. "You've got to see it; you've got to see it" She kept reminding me we had just driven 20 hours straight, had little sleep, and were now ascending an incline at 8,500 feet above sea level.

About halfway up, I saw something descending the trail at a very rapid speed. As we were in the middle of a national forest, I considered the possibility of a wild animal. Having experienced quite a bit of wildlife in previous years at Quaker Ridge, I knew a bear or mountain lion wouldn't be good company.

Bounding down the trail, however, was a 12-year-old boy. Taking giant steps, he was on the verge of losing total control as he rifled down the mountainside. About 50 feet in front of me, he yelled, "Are you Jay Laffoon?" I said, "Yes." Now 20 feet past me, he yelled over his shoulder "GOOOOOOOD!" not even breaking stride.

My best friend in the world was Dean Moyer, a college bud who moved to Atlanta to work for the same now defunct company. He had phoned ahead and arranged for a single red rose to be delivered to the foot of the cross on the top of the mountain. The attached card read, "Congratulations Jay and Laura, Love, Dean." Laura arrived at the cross first, saw the rose and said in her sweet southern drawl. "Hey, there's a flower…" "Pick it up," I replied.

"Oh, it has a card…"

"Well, read it."

"Oh my goodness…it says 'Congratulations, Jay and Laura, Love, Dean.' What do you suppose that means?"

My plan was unraveling before my eyes, I had to think quickly. "Uhhhh, maybe Dean was just congratulating us on climbing the mountain." I paused, waiting for a reply, hoping she bought my story.

"Ohhh isn't that sweet, how nice."

Woosh…right over her head.

The pizza was now 40 minutes cold and the champagne warm (I had convinced Laura it was a bottle I'd saved for a special picnic). We had just gotten out of our car and climbed over a thousand feet to the top of this 8500-foot mountain. Laura and I sat with our legs dangling over the edge of the cliff with the cross right above us. We looked out over the marvelous landscape drenched in the noontime sun. It was time!

I reached in the backpack, pulled out the ring box, opened it, and held my hands toward Laura. "Honey, I know I've asked you this, and I know you said yes, but I just want to make it official. Will you marry me?"

At that moment Laura's bottom lip began to quiver (I now know what that quiver means). At first, it was cute, and then sweat began to bead up on her forehead. I couldn't ever remember seeing her sweat; after all, it's not dignified for a southern girl to sweat (and I also now know what that sweat means). The look on her face was puzzling as if she was caught halfway between ecstasy and agony (And I now know what that look means).

Nothing came out of her mouth for what seemed like an eternity. So again I asked, "Honey, will you marry me?"

At that moment, the word "Yes" did not come out of her mouth. The word "No" did not come out of her mouth. But something did come start coming out of her mouth. This woman I loved, this woman I was asking to marry me, this woman I wanted to spend the rest of my life with began to spew an uninterrupted stream of pizza, champagne, and gastrointestinal juices all over me. All I could think was, "Does this mean Yes?"

She could have puked over the edge of the cliff, or she could have turned her head the other way, but no, she had to barf all over me. Immediately she began to laugh, but I was failing to see the humor. Slowly a smile crept over my face as she put the ring on her finger and hugged me all covered with goo. "YES, YES, YES, YES, YES! Don't you know in the South a woman must puke on a man before she can marry him?"

We wiped the remains off the corners of her mouth and off the front of my clothes. I will never forget that day, or...that smell. Let the celebration begin!

One

You Gotta
Laugh

*I*t was Friday night; Laura and I had worked an incredibly hard week. At 11:00 my head hit the pillow and I was out like a light. At 11:06, Laura nudged me under the covers. Instantly, there was an unconscious smile on my face. I didn't care how tired I was, this was great news! With this thought racing through my mind, I was totally taken off guard when Laura whispered, "Jay, someone's in the house." At first I couldn't comprehend it. My mind was thinking a very happy thought, and my wife was saying, "Someone's in the house."

We had lived in this house just over a month and a half. It was our first home and we were proud as peacocks. The only furniture we possessed were hand-me-downs from our parents, but this home was ours. Two weeks before this fabled Friday night, three inmates—two rapists and a murderer—had escaped from the federal prison in Atlanta. The rapists were caught the very next day, but the murderer was still on the loose.

This fugitive's mode of operation was to hide out in the woods of Atlanta during the day and break into homes while the occupants were at work or school. He would steal food, clothing, anything he could find to make his way out of town under the cover of darkness. The media was all over this story with "sightings" of him here and there, and they were actually tracking the sightings in the vicinity of our little subdivision in Snellville.

Earlier in the week Laura and I had come home to find police cars all over our street. Our neighbor's home across the street was burglarized, though all that was taken was food and clothing.

Through half open eyes, I rolled my head over and peered, hoping to get a clearer picture of what my wife was saying. Laura had pulled the covers over her head, so all I could see was her mouth, nose, and two eyes the size of silver dollar pancakes. She whisper screamed at me, "Jay, someone's in the house. Go get him!" I shot straight up in bed, my heart pounding out 145 beats a minute, fueled by the instantaneous flow of adrenaline now coursing through my veins. My ears felt as big as satellite dishes as I quietly turned my head back and forth waiting. Thump! Thump!

Women just don't understand men when it comes to crisis. Young boys dream about opportunities like this. The newspaper headlines will tell the world of our heroic act of bravery. I knew two things: 1) This murderer was in my house, and 2) He was going down.

Well, that's the fantasy. Reality...I was closer to Barney Fife than Rambo. I fell out of bed, shaking and stumbling around as I made my way to our closet and did the one thing I told myself I would never, never do: I got out the shotgun.

Tiptoeing to the door of our bedroom, I chambered a shell "Chechunk" and said in the deepest baritone voice I could muster, "Laura, call the cops!"

I wanted this murderer to think I was a six-foot-eight, 400-pound gorilla of a man coming after him with an 8-gauge elephant gun. In reality, I was a five-foot-nine pudgy wimp with a 4/10 my grandpa had given me when I turned 12.

We lived in a tri-level house with three bedrooms and two bathrooms upstairs. Five steps down was the living room, turn the corner, and down five more into the dining room/kitchen. The one car garage/laundry room was located just off the kitchen. I searched all the upstairs bedrooms first. (The bedrooms with no furniture or no pictures.) Poking the gun into the room I flicked on the light with the barrel and crouched into the ready position I had witnessed on so many TV action dramas.

No one in our bedroom or bath, no one in the first extra bedroom, same for the second. I reached the extra bathroom and noticed the shower curtain was closed. I had vivid memories of all those "Psycho" movies as the barrel of the gun whisked back the curtain. No one in the shower. (Laura had closed the curtain, unbeknown to me).

I stood at the top of the stairs for what seemed like hours, knowing that if I crept down the stairs, "he" could ambush me easily. I figured my only chance was surprise. One, two, three, jump…AHHHHHHHH! I hit the floor, did a perfect roll, and got up ready to shoot anything that moved.

In the corner of the living room was an old TV, the kind that used picture tubes instead of microchips, and glowed even after you turned them off. My mind, seeing the glow, told me there was an alien in the corner of my living room. Luckily a slow trigger finger saved the life of that old TV. I was ready to blow it away, right then and there.

I checked behind the couch, behind the loveseat, behind the old black-duct-taped together vinyl Lazyboy my dad had reluctantly given us. "That's the best chair in the house!" he insisted, as he pleaded his case to Mom. Mom won…Mom always wins. I was so paranoid, I even checked the chimney as the famed "San Francisco Santa Claus" murders came to mind.

Then I did the Rambo jump/roll thing into the dining room, banging my head on a chair. Checked the pantry, the fridge, made myself a quick snack. Checked the garage. Nobody!

Meanwhile, I had turned on every light in the house, every light outside the house. We looked like the Griswalds in the "Christmas Vacation" movie.

Only slightly coming to my senses, I made my way back up to the living room. Our house was located on a cul-de-sac, and a large bay window in our living room provided a perfect view of our neighbors front porch—our neighbors who were having a party. As I watched their guests leave and slam their car doors, I noticed the familiar sound I had heard in bed—Thump, thump! For a moment I was relieved, the adrenaline pump subsided, and I stood there stunned at all the fuss. At that same moment, my neighbors came out onto their porch with the last guests of the evening, and their eyes naturally were drawn to my fully illuminated house.

I will never forget the look on that our neighbor lady's face. Alfalfa from "The Little Rascals" is as close as I can come to describing it. Her hair looked like it was standing straight up on end. Her eyes were as big as dinner plates, and she stood there flapping her husband on the shoulder with the back of her hand. With hands in his pockets, he slowly shook his head back and forth, back and forth.

Suddenly, I realized the problem. All the lights inside and outside our house were on. Complicating the matter, I'm standing in this big bay window with my shotgun in my hand! I felt like a fool, a big dumb stupid fool. Trying to remain calm, I slowly lowered the gun. At that moment, the cold steel of the barrel hit my stomach, and I realized that not only was I standing in this window, in our fully illuminated house with my shotgun in my hand, but I was head to toe, naked!

Instead of simply dropping to the floor, I actually spent about 12 seconds trying to hide behind the shotgun! Have you ever tried to hide a 210-pound naked body behind a shotgun? Don't. It doesn't work.

Finally, coming to my senses, I dropped to the floor and did the "Bugs Bunny" slither back up the stairs. Upon reaching the door of our bedroom, I snarled, "Laura, (chechunk went the gun) you are in deep weeds!"

We spent the next day laughing about our paranoia. Heck, we'll spend the rest of our lives laughing at that one.

For some reason, our neighbor wouldn't let his kids play in our yard after that night.

"Lucy, Lucy, Lucy, you got some 'splanin' to do." Any fan of the "I Love Lucy" show will quickly recognize those famous words that came from Ricky's mouth almost every week as Lucy got herself into yet another mess. As Americans watched the Ricardos week after week, we saw in them a couple who could make us laugh, as well as laugh at themselves.

Laughter has been life giving in our marriage! Like air and water, we would not have been able to survive without it. We have always been able to laugh at each other—that's the easy part. We have also had to learn to laugh at ourselves.

For us laughter has changed the course of many arguments. Laughter has started out many days on a bright note. Laughter has changed many sorrowful moments into wonderful memories. It is a must in any marriage. It's a survival technique.

We have discovered four truths about laughter.

Laughter Changes Your Chemistry

Most people understand that our bodies are little chemical factories. Every day hundreds of different chemicals course through our bloodstream, our lymph system, and every other part of our body. Literally, without these chemicals, our bodies would not—and could not—exist.

Laura and Her Dad

I was a typical girl growing up in a typical family in Atlanta, Georgia. At least, that's what I thought. I was ten years old before I realized that my daddy was not like other daddies. My daddy was from Grantville, a very small town an hour south of Atlanta. At the age of six, he contracted polio, then, in his young adult years, he was diagnosed with diabetes. He was a good man who seemed to get knocked down in life every time he turned around.

I am the youngest girl and the third of four children, two boys and two girls. Early in my life, I can remember my daddy running and playing with us as much as any other daddy. But there came a point when our lives changed and he couldn't do a lot of that anymore. By the time I was 15, he had suffered four heart attacks and three strokes, and was no longer a healthy man. Early in my teenage years, the doctor put him on an array of medications for his physical and emotional health.

One day I came home from school and found him sitting in his favorite Lazyboy chair with a blanket pulled over his head! "Dad, are you awake?" He responded by nodding his head. I could only see the blanket move. From that point on, every day was the same. He would sit for hours at a time in that chair with that silly blanket over his head. I thought he had finally gone crazy. I know I would have if I had experienced all the hard knocks in life that he had.

Actually, my daddy was experiencing what is now known as a chemical imbalance, due to the various medications he was taking reacting with his body. The chemicals were so out of balance they caused him to be lethargic and unable to think clearly.

The natural chemicals in our bodies have a great amount of power. Scientists tell us that a variety of emotions can release different chemicals into our bloodstream. It is widely accepted that one of the reasons people train for endurance athletic events like running and biking is to experience an "endorphin rush" that follows the event or training.

These same "endorphins" are released when a person laughs. Understand, we are not talking about a mere chuckle or a snicker. We mean a laugh, an all-out, make-your-belly-shake-laugh. It doesn't have to be long, but it does need to be a laugh. Like a powerful drug, endorphins soothe and comfort. Some say they even promote healing. Think about that. When you laugh, you could actually be helping your body heal itself.

The healing properties of laughter go far beyond the body.

Jay Travels to Romania

I was in Romania with a large group of U.S military kids. Leaving my family and traveling halfway around the world, I was privileged to be with these teens on their spring break as they participated with a group called Military Community Youth Ministry

(MCYM). During the day, these kids would complete work projects in and around the city of Arad, Romania. At night, we met with our teenage Romanian interpreters—nearly 1,000 of us in all.

As I presented Christ to these kids, I began the evening with a little comedy. Each night, a different Romanian young person would approach me saying, "Jay, I haven't laughed like that in my entire life." This may seem like a simple cliché to Americans, but for these kids, it was the truth. Their world is very different from our American life, and true laughter is not all that common. The healing power of laughter goes beyond the body and touches the soul.

In marriage, laughter can change the chemistry of a day, it can change the mood around the dinner table, and it can also promote balance in a healthy sexual relationship.

Laughter in the Bedroom?

As a man, there are many nights when I enter the bedroom with a certain agenda. Unfortunately, Laura often seems to have a much different agenda—sleep! Early in our marriage, I would fuss and fume under the covers as my advances seemed to fall unheeded. Then, one night for reasons I still do not remember, instead of fussing and fuming, I started to tickle Laura. For the next 20 to 30 minutes we laughed and tickled and played with each other like we hadn't done in years. When we were done, Laura rolled over and coyly asked, "Was it good for you?" I had to admit it was fantastic!

Those now frequent (okay, maybe once or twice a month) bedroom-laughing parties have added a tremendous boost to our other nighttime activities.

Laughter changes your chemistry!

Laughter Changes Your Attitude

It has been said that a true sense of humor is not one's ability to laugh as anyone can do that. A true sense of humor is one's ability to laugh at oneself.

Laura's Irritation

If you were to ask me, "Laura, what is the one thing about Jay that irritates you?" I would have to answer, "His ability to laugh in the middle of an argument!"

We will be fussing and fuming, arguing and yelling, and with no warning at all, this big grin comes across his face, one of those grins that you can't help but grin yourself.

"But I am in the middle of an argument," my brain says to my face.

"Don't grin," responds my brain. It wants to be mad. There is a war going on between my ears. And then he does it! He laughs. It is all over. My brain gives in. I laugh.

I don't want to laugh, I am mad. About what? I can't remember, but I am mad.

My brain is on overload. I think I am mad, but my face is refusing to respond with anger. My face is grinning, not an angry response. My brain shuts down. The argument is over. I can't remember why I was arguing and yelling anyway, so I might as well give up.

Attitude is so important. The following is an excerpt from a piece on attitude penned by Chuck Swindoll:

The longer I live,
the more I realize the impact of attitude on life.
Attitude, to me, is more important
than what other people think or say or do.
It is more important than appearance, giftedness or skill.
The remarkable thing is we have a choice every day regarding the
attitude we will embrace for that day.
We cannot change our past.
We cannot change the fact that people
will act in a certain way.
I am convinced that
life is 10 percent what happens to me
and 90 percent how I react to it.

In marriage there is probably nothing as important as attitude. Growing up, I was a boy who got too upset over little things. Mom would always ask, "Will this thing you're getting mad about matter in 100 years? If the answer is yes, then your anger is justified. If the answer is no, then move on. It's not worth getting worked up over.

What sensible advice. Yes, there are some issues in marriage that will matter in 100 years—issues like infidelity, parenting, and your spiritual life. But, there are far too many issues that won't matter in 100 years, things like dinner being late or the toilet seat being left up. Our attitude about these "little" things will have a tremendous impact on our marriages.

The ability to step back and laugh at ourselves will help change us, and the ensuing laughter will provide some great memories. Laughter changes your attitude.

Laughter Changes Your Perspective

Growing up as the son of a youth minister certainly had its perks. For example, since 1973 I have spent time in Colorado every summer except for two occasions when getting off work was not possible.

I understand the privilege of visiting a place touched by the hand of God. Quaker Ridge Camp was and remains an incredible experience for all who accept the challenge. Very few opportunities change your life like a Rocky Mountain camping experience.

Over the years, I have gained an appreciation for the mountains, Pikes Peak in particular. Without a doubt, one of those life-changing experiences for me has been to gaze year after year upon this magnificent mountain.

More recently I almost feel the mountain speaking to me, though every year it seems to repeat the same theme or anthem.

Pikes Peak, at 14,110 feet, is an unusual mountain in that you can drive to the summit where a gift and coffee shop are located. To sit on what the senses tell you is the top of the world and sip coffee, eat the world's best donuts, and buy over-priced T-shirts is a wild experience unlike any other. When you ascend Pikes Peak, the mountain speaks to you…and to everyone who will pause and listen. For some, the altitude will make your head feel lighter than usual and your stomach ache. For others, a quick descent—carefully maneuvering the curves and switchbacks of Pikes Peak highway—is the only remedy for the inevitable sickness. The view takes your breath away, and the mountain's words leave you awestruck and filled with wonder as you gaze upon mile after mile of land spanning the horizon.

For me it's different. I haven't tackled the summit of Pikes Peak in more than five years. But every year I'm in Colorado, Pikes Peak speaks to me and the words get louder: "Hey there, puny little man, it is so good to see you again. That's right, I'm still here. You see I've been here for a very long time, longer than you can even imagine. Oh, and by the way, I'll be here when you are nothing but dust. Sure, you can put holes in me and build your little road so people can reach my summit, but you, my little friend, will never see the end of me. I will remain long after the memory of you!"

Man, does that hurt! Grasping that concept changes my outlook. Every year I leave Colorado with a new and different personal perspective of life.

Laughter can perform that same metamorphosis in a marriage. Martin Luther once stated, "I judge the depth of a man's faith by his ability to laugh." How true.

In marriage, there are times when issues arise that *will* make a difference in 100 years. Those issues cannot be solved with laughter. The solution lies in hard work and faith in a God that is more powerful than any issue. Only He can transport you and your spouse to the other side of any problem.

Imagine yourself in the middle of a storm. Hear the thunder. See the lightning. Feel the howling wind. See the trees bending beyond what is natural. Note the rain coming down so hard you can't see your hand in front of your face. All of a sudden, the reflection you see is startling. A picture of yourself. You look like a drowned rat. Your hair is plastered to your head. Black mascara streams down your face. Your shirt sleeves hang lengthened by the weight of the soaked fabric. Your pants cling to your legs. This vivid image may induce laughter. For a moment the storm has lost its ability to terrify you. From this perspective, the storm doesn't seem so life-threatening after all. Laughter in the middle of those stormy arguments can give you a broader perspective—a higher view. The result: the issue has lost its power. Laughter isn't going to make problems disappear anymore than it can make a storm disappear, but it can change how you view the storm. Ultimately, laughter changes your perspective.

Laughter Changes Your Heart

In Proverbs 4:23 Solomon reminds us, "Above all else, guard your heart, for it is the wellspring of life" (NIV).

Ever wonder what life would be like without feelings? Life void of anger and rage, and no one getting their feelings hurt over a few choice words that slip out unintentionally. Only when we imagine the bad feelings gone, does life appears appealing.

What we would miss, however, is unimaginable. Emotions drive, motivate, and prod us to act and react to the world around us every day. That is why Solomon encouraged us to guard our hearts as he realized this is where the essence of life originates. An understanding of this concept becomes doubly important in marriage because we are guarding not only our heart but also the hearts of our spouse and children.

Take, for example, our sexual drives. As we will discuss in a later chapter, sex for men is a strong physical urge that may appear void of romance or feeling. Nothing could be further from the truth for women. In most cases, sex is all about feelings, emotions, and the state of their heart. An old saying can help us gain some perspective: "For a man, when all is right in the bedroom, all is right with the world. For a woman, when all is right with the world, all is right in the bedroom." A woman's heart, revealed by her emotions, plays a large role in all that she is and does.

This is why many women are attracted to men who can make them laugh.

Gene and Wendy are good friends with whom we've enjoyed many endearing experiences. When we first moved to Alma, we bought their house—the house of Wendy's childhood. We now share a new neighborhood. Gene "Mister Meticulous," as he is known, is a CPA with a dry sense of humor bordering on perpetual sarcasm. He is really very funny!

We love him, though other people often don't know when Gene is serious or when he is joking around.

Wendy is a sweet innocent woman who would never be caught saying an unkind word about anyone. She is Gene's biggest fan! When he gets on a roll, cracking jokes, Wendy splits her gut with contagious laughter! So even when you aren't sure whether Gene is joking or not, you will laugh with Wendy, because her husband always makes her laugh.

Laughter helps us forget about the troubles that surround us. Laughter literally reaches deep within us and changes our heart.

In Proverbs 17:22 Solomon wrote, "A cheerful heart is good medicine, but a crushed spirit dries up the bones" (NIV). When laughter becomes an integral part of our marriage, we expose our lives to a healing power that will help us realize the potential growth God intended us to experience as a couple. When we intentionally build times of laughter into our lives, it is like taking a daily swig of castor oil—without the lousy taste. We begin to experience all of the benefits and less pain.

Laughter changes your body chemistry. Laughter changes your attitude. Laughter changes your perspective. Laughter changes your heart. So remember, "You gotta laugh."

Why not . . .

+ Spend some time recalling some humorous moments in your marriage.
+ Take in a funny movie or play.
+ Create your own video comedy marathon.
+ Read funny books together.
+ Have a laughing party at the dinner table.

Two

You Gotta
L o v e

*S*orry, but love is not like a box of chocolates. It's more like a mountain that will frustrate, stun, and amaze all at the same time.

Salvation Army Meets Mt. Everest

The story is told of a young Salvation Army officer who had always wanted to see Mt. Everest. On his pay, however, it was just a dream—that is, until one day a position opened for a Salvation Army captain in India, near Nepal. He applied for the position and was soon on his way.

Upon arriving at his post, he began to plan and save for the trip of a lifetime to see mighty Everest. After nearly two years of planning and saving, he was ready. He began his trip by taking a train to Katmandu, Nepal, where he connected with his guide who would take him the rest of the way. A heavy fog began to settle and the captain became a little discouraged as the mountain range he dreamed of seeing was covered in an eerie white.

The captain and the guide drove the Jeep for hours over roads that could barely be called paths. As time passed, the fog seemed to thicken and the captain began to think his trip might be in vain. But the guide simply said, "Continue."

Soon the fog turned to snow. The change was sudden and severe and the captain urged the guide to turn back. "Continue," was all the guide would say. After many hours of driving in the dark, the guide parked the Jeep and the two men spent the night at a lodge. Actually it was more of a one-room shack with beds, but it was a place to sleep.

The next morning they awoke to almost two feet of fresh snow with more falling by the second. The captain became agitated, frustrated and bordered on belligerent, but again, the guide simply said, "Continue." They began their difficult hike. The captain complained and threatened to turn back many times; each time the guide said, "Continue."

Slowly, as the snow began to taper, the captain stopped and strained to see if he could catch even a glimpse of the outline of a mountain, any mountain. More hiking, more complaining. The snow had stopped, but the cloud cover was still very thick. Finally the guide stopped, turned to the captain and announced, "Your mountain, sir."

"Where?" cried the captain. "Where?!" At that moment the guide put a finger to the chin of the captain and raised his head to the sky. There in all its majesty and splendor, was Everest, looming above the clouds like a prince in a parade. The captain fell back, gasped for breath, and shook his head. No words came to his lips, no expression sufficed. He was in awe and he would never be the same.

Love can have that same effect. It can leave us speechless, grasping for words that won't come and shaking our heads knowing we cannot describe what is happening to us. We will never be the same.

Love is the expression we show toward others when we are living in the presence of God. In 1 John we read "God is love. Whoever lives in love lives in God, and God in him" (4:8,16 NIV). God is the one true source of love and when we love our spouse, we are showing them a glimpse of the love of God. You can express your love for your spouse in the following ways.

Express Your Love Through Intimacy

When we stood at the altar on that memorable day and said "I do," how many of us can say honestly that we knew what love was? For some it was an ooey gooey feeling in the pit of our stomach. For others it was the hormones that drove us crazy. As Jay and I began our life together, I can remember clearly thinking that I had married an "animal." Our views on intimate life were at opposite ends of the spectrum. For me, intimacy was all about taking walks together, eating together, shopping together. He was all about...well, you know what he was all about!

I grew up in a very proper southern home. The word "sex" was non-existent. Now, I had married a man who thought about it all the time. As we deliberated on how to communicate our differing needs to one another, Jay expressed a word picture to illustrate his point of view. "Laura, sex to me is like the air I breathe." I promptly told him to go find an oxygen tank!

Needless to say, intimacy is a huge issue in every marriage. One of us desires affection more than the other; one desires sexual intimacy more than the other. Our appetites and tastes are very different. (By the way, when I get to heaven one of my first questions is going to be why God made men and women such complete opposites!)

I have a word picture that may make these differences easier to grasp. Gentlemen, wives are like Crock-Pots. We're like slow cookers, that take time to cook—sometimes all day. First thing in the morning we need to be connected to the power source, and let us cook all day. Understand though, that if you unplug the Crock-Pot through harsh words or actions, you may have to start all over...tomorrow! Men, However, are microwaves. You just punch in the time and they are ready to go!

Generally speaking (but not always), it is the woman who desires affection and the man who desires sexual intimacy. They are both expressions of intimate love in our marriage.

For a woman, affection comes in many forms. I am not a touch feely person. My needs do not include having Jay hold my hand or put his arm around me. From my perspective, my husband displays his affection by spending time with me. Dr. Gary Chapman identifies the concept of love language in his book, The Five Languages of Love. Each of us communicates by means of a different love language. My love language is quality time. Jay's is physical touch. We highly recommend this book as a tool to discover the love language you and your spouse prefer.

Answer this question: What is it that you do for your spouse when you want to show him love? My preference is to buy Jay a gift or suggest we do something together such as golfing or running. I speak my love language to Jay, the language I understand. When Jay expresses love to me, he does it by holding my hand or giving me a hug. He is speaking through his love language of physical touch. For years in our marriage we both thought we were showing love to the other. The fact of the matter was, that while we were each genuine in our intentions, we weren't speaking love in a language the recipient could easily identify.

The answer to the question "What do I do to show love?" is a clue to your love language. Your spouse's answer is a clue to their love language. The key is discovering how your spouse needs to feel loved and then help each other communicate in that way. It will seem foreign to you at first, but it will speak volumes to your spouse.

I had just returned from a five-day road trip and was relieved to be home and return to some routine tasks. I love to play basketball and often indulge myself at a local community center. At 11:30 the next morning I skipped out the door, giving Laura a quick peck on the cheek (more on this in chapter 3). At noon Laura entered the gym. I took a time out to find out what had brought her to the community center. " Hey Jay, would you like to go out for lunch?" "No," I replied. "I'm enjoying the game." Laura's face should have sent flares off in my mind, but I turned back toward the court, took two steps, and froze.

Laura wasn't asking me if I was hungry or wanted lunch; she was asking me if I loved her. To her, going out to lunch was the best way I could communicate that I missed her the past week and wanted nothing more than spend time with her. Quickly calculating that if I wanted her to show me how much she "missed" me later that evening, then I'd better grab my stuff and catch her before she could leave the parking lot. Lunch was great and so was the evening. We still laugh when we think of that day and how, for the first time, I actually realized what preparations were necessary to get Laura "cooking."

Express Love Through Communication

"You learn more about someone through an hour of play than through an hour of conversing" –Plato

As a young lady embarking on your dating life, remember how you became avidly interested in the activities in which your boyfriend participated. You may have never attended a sporting event in your life, but if that particular fellow liked sports, you liked sports.

Why? Because we all seek companionship in relationships. We seek someone with whom we can play and enjoy life. When we marry, we feel we have found that someone. All too often that becomes less of a priority as we live our daily lives. It is as if when we stand at the altar and say "I do" to love, honor and cherish, we say "I don't" to sports, hunting, cars, or whatever activity embodies our husband's passion. We begin to live our lives as separate entities. As we speak to married couples, we often hear, "He does his thing, and I do mine."

All of us share a need to commune with others. We desire communication with another human, on a more intimate level than merely the superficial details of family life. One reason women have girlfriends to have lunch or shop with, and men have golfing or hunting buddies, is that when we play, we communicate on a different level.

Seek activities that you and your spouse can do together, that you both enjoy, and "play" together. This is a great way to connect (communicate) to the body, mind, and soul of your mate.

Social scientists tell us that the average man speaks 10,000 words a day while the average woman speaks 20,000. Generally speaking, women require conversation more than men. When "Mr." comes home from a long day at the office, after speaking 9,996 words throughout the day, he walks in the door, says, "Hi honey, I'm home," and thus fulfilled his quota. "Mrs." on the other hand is just getting started. Even if she has had a long day at the office or at home, she's probably still only spent half her quota!

This is why it is vital that most men improve their listening skills. It amazes me as I speak to businessmen across the country how many of them want to improve their sales skills or presentation skills, but can't translate those same skills to the home. To be a good conversationalist, you have to ask open-ended questions. Don't ask questions that can be answered yes or no.

Start your question with the phrase, "Tell me about..." or, "How do you feel about...?", then sit back and let your wife use up some of her 20,000 words. Don't get me wrong, however. Open-ended questions are not a magic pill; you still have to genuinely care about what your wife is saying. It is important to pay attention, focus on your spouse and respond to her. Let her feel that you hear what she is trying to communicate.

Expressing Love Through Service

I call it the "Father Knows Best" syndrome. Every man deep down inside dreams of coming home to a spotless house, the aroma of fresh baked bread wafting through the air, children playing quietly, and his chair, newspaper, slippers, and remote control all ready for him.

Poof! Busted your bubble! Welcome to the real world, buddy!

We might all love to have life work like that but, in truth, it is nestled somewhere between "Father Knows Best" and "Roseanne"! Yet, all have a need to be served. This isn't the idea of wait-on-me-hand-and-foot service. It is rather an understanding that someone loves you when they serve you, in whatever capacity.

In the last 30 years we have seen women run from any type of title that might suggest domesticity. "Domestic" is defined as "of the home." What we need to understand is that our husbands have a need for us to serve through "management" of the home.

Hey, sit back down and keep on reading. Don't leave yet, hear me out.

This does not mean that you must do all the cooking, cleaning, and caring for the children. It does mean that the wife is the "general contractor of the home." I believe God designed us with this capability. Women, in general, can do more than one thing at a time (in computer terms this is called "multi-tasking") most men cannot. Their brains are more compartmentalized, more focused on one thing at a time. Women possess cerebral crossover. The female left brain can talk to the right brain and vice versa. Taking care of the home, or being the general contractor, involves managing many tasks simultaneously.

At a job site a general contractor delegates tasks to subcontractors. Our job site is our home and we must delegate the jobs necessary to keep our family organized and to meet everyone's needs. We oversee the work and yes, at times, we do perform many of the tasks. After all, as the general contractor we are the experts!

Not only do our husbands need our service in our homes, but also, if applicable, we must be general contractor of our children. We must manage their schedules, their chores, their school work, and so on. Again, I am not saying we are required to do the tasks, but we take responsibility for managing the functions. "Jay, tonight Torrey needs to be at soccer practice at 6:00. I need you to take him."

Have you seen the credit card commercial where the wife has spent all day with the kids. That evening she and her husband go out for dinner and the only language she verbalizes is "Barney, the purple dinosaur" language? I can really identify with this scenario! This is another area where we can serve our husbands. Not only do our bodies require proper sleep, nutrition, and exercise, but social and mental outlets as well. Read a newspaper or check out the headlines on the internet. Have lunch with friends on a regular basis. Attend an exercise class or join a gym.

The general contractor needs to be in good form in order to get the job done. It may mean being a little selfish at times and taking time for yourself, but we have the most important job in the universe. As wives and mothers we need the energy resources to complete the job to the glory of the Lord!

I am convinced that despite what Hollywood would have us believe, most ladies would rather have time with their husbands than more money. Also, I believe they would choose their husbands' presence over their presents. As our good friend Ken Davis shares, love is spelled T.I.M.E. When we give of our time, we serve our wives and children.

"Show me your checkbook and I'll show you your priorities!" I remember hearing a preacher say these words during stewardship season (that time of year the church sets aside to discuss finances). Scripture bears this out: "For where your treasure is, there your heart will be also." Luke 12:34 (NIV) While the statement my pastor made is still true today, I believe a better statement would be, "Show me your Day-Timer or Palm Pilot and I'll show you your priorities." Americans have discovered that there are only 24 hours in a day, and with all of our modern conveniences and time-saving devices we still struggle to prioritize our time.

Plan time to be with your spouse, your kids, and your family, however big or small. It's a matter of service to them, and is an unquestionable expression of love that will lead to celebration.

Express Love Through Respect

I am married to a firstborn son, and a firstborn grandson, on both sides—a golden child. His mother always told him he could do whatever he set his mind to, and he believed it. When we were married, I thought my primary calling was to keep this man humble. I have the gift of verbal attack (not really abuse, just a quick wit and razor sharp tongue). I proceeded for the next ten years to take this calling very seriously.

An incident that happened in 1995, however, showed me that maybe I had read the wrong job description. Jay was preparing to board a flight to Miami where he was going to train some urban youth leaders and it hit me what he was doing with his life. I had watched him over the last few years struggle and wrestle with his life dream to be a speaker. We had worked in Youth for Christ for over ten years, and were beginning to feel God's leading elsewhere. Jay was boarding a plane to follow God's calling, his dream.

They announced his flight so it was time to say good-bye. I kissed him and said these words, "Honey, I am proud of you," and he walked down the jet way to his plane.

That evening he called to let us know that he had arrived safely and told me that he had entered the plane blubbering like an idiot because of me! I was offended! What did I say? What did I do? He said, "Laura, in the ten years we have been married, you have never told me you were proud of me." Wow! I read the job description wrong!

Ladies, our job is not to keep our husband humble. That is the Lord's job. Our job is to make sure that our husbands have what they need from us to face a cruel and angry world. They need our admiration. I've heard it said, "Behind every great man is a woman who thinks he hung the moon." Another favorite is, "Be to his faults very blind, to his virtues very kind."

Your husband needs you to express your love for him through admiration, and give him the respect he needs to conquer the giants in his world. He may not always be admirable, but our role is still to love him, admire him, and let the Lord humble him.

Men are taught not to show their feelings. Hold it in, be tough, and don't show anyone your cards! Along comes the latter part of the twentieth century and now men are called to be emotional, to express their feelings. Oh, it is all so confusing!

I've come across one word that really works for me; maybe it will for you, too. It's transparent—be transparent with your wife. Most women know the kind of man they married. They know if you are the strong silent type or the emotional guy who cries in movies. Either way, they aren't looking for you to be someone you aren't. They are looking to see the real you twenty-four hours a day, seven days a week.

We express our love through respect when we include our wives in all aspects of our lives. Our transparency allows our wife to see when we are happy, sad, angry, or filled with anticipation. It is through that transparency that we help them feel a part of our lives outside of the home.

An old song says that people will know we are Christians by our love. Great words. Not only does our world need to see

Christian individuals who love but, more importantly, our world needs to see husbands and wives who love. The unbelieving world needs to see men and women who don't have it "all together," yet love each other in spite of their deficiencies. When we express our love through intimacy, conversation, service, and respect, our marriages will be a testimony to the world around us.

Why not . . .

+ Converse about the expressions of love. Do they ring true?

+ Evaluate yourself and your spouse on how well you express love.

+ Set a realistic goal—one "expression" that needs work. What specifically can be done to improve this phase of your marriage?

Three

You Gotta
Listen

*W*hen our son, Torrey was born, we couldn't wait for him to talk! We would get in his face and do that eager parent thing: "Torrey, can you say 'mommy'?" We were sure we had a genius for a son when he started talking at eight months. TJ has been talking our ears off ever since! Most days he can keep us mesmerized with his stories of inventions and adventures. Then there are days the questions come so fast and furious, we wonder if our brains will explode.

Marriages experience eagerness similar to that of new parents wishing that their child could talk. When the child finally does, we wish then that he would just quit talking for awhile and listen! Most of us start our marriages desiring so much for our spouses to communicate with us, to tell us what they're feeling, what they dream and desire. Then when they do, we find ourselves wanting them to stop and listen to *our* dreams and desires instead.

A few summers ago, Jay and I were in Findlay, Ohio, doing a marriage seminar for a large family conference sponsored by the Church of God. One afternoon during the week, we had some free time to enjoy our favorite pastime, golf. Ken Davis happened to be the keynote speaker at this conference and he and Jay thought it would be fun for all of us to go golfing together. Ken's son-in-law, Brian, was traveling with Ken. So here I go golfing with three men!

Now, I was just beginning to enjoy golf and was outwardly cocky enough to think this would be fun, while on the inside I was terrified that I was going to make a fool of myself on the course. The first five holes went well and then the swing broke down. (That is golfer's lingo for having a "Jerry Lewis attack.") I could not hit the ball and when I did connect, it went in the opposite direction of the intended destination. The ball flew into the weeds, the creek, the trees…everywhere but on the fairway! Somehow I finally managed to get the ball on the green using seven strokes on a par three hole! That means that in a perfect world, it should only take me three shots to actually land the ball onto the green and into the hole. Instead, I had already hit the ball seven times and was just now on the green, and had to still putt the ball! I believe I walked off the sixth green with a ten. I slumped into the golf cart dejected and embarrassed. Jay turned to me and said, "You gotta put the bad holes behind you and play on."

I became hysterical! "Fine, if I am such a bad golfer you don't have to play with me anymore! I am sorry I embarrassed you in front of your friends. Just let me drive the cart!"

What Jay said and what I heard were two completely different things! He had not called me a bad golfer. He was actually trying to encourage me to forget about it and play on. What I heard was entirely different. I heard him say I was a bad golfer and not worthy of playing. Sound ridiculous!? Yes, but don't we all do this in our marriages?

It is hard work to communicate, especially in marriage. Your ability to communicate effectively will make or break your marriage. First, you must understand the many different types of communication you can have in a single day, then practice each type on a regular basis.

Marital communication is much like a house. Every room in your home is unique. It is decorated different and has different functions and purposes as you move through your day.

Think of communication like moving from room to room in your house. In each room of the house various types of communication occur. Just as we use each room in our home on a regular basis, there will be times when we use each type of communication on a daily basis. Now, you may not have each type of room in your home, but you will need to employ all of these forms of communication in order to *celebrate*. You can improve your marriage by successfully communicating in every room of your house.

The Living Room—
Communication Through Planning

For us, a special time of the day is morning when we have our family devotion time. It is the time we spiritually "plan" our day by starting it off with the Lord.

Family devotions at our home began when Torrey could sit still long enough to look at the colorful pictures in his *Children's Bible*. These devotional moments are never long, but are filled with nuggets of truth and memories for a lifetime.

I realized the impact of our routine one day when Torrey was about four. I had asked him to retrieve something from the living room. He was a little confused by my directions and finally asked, "Dad, is it by your chair in the devotion room?" At that moment, I knew that what we did each day in that room was an integral part of his day. Never underestimate the importance of a few moments spent wisely. Your living room is a great place to show your spouse and children the importance of day-to-day conversation with God.

Some couples have devotions together, we cannot. Jay and I are just enough different in the books we choose to read and the way in which we have our devotions that it has never meshed for us. We have our devotions at the same time, but we read and study different topics. Then we take time to discuss the nourishment we received while studying and share about what the Lord is teaching us. Sometimes we share answers to prayer and present needs about which we would like the other to pray.

The Plan

"Hey Dad, what's the plan for today?"

That question is heard over and over at the Laffoon house while little ears are waiting to see when Mom or Dad is available for some playtime. For us, "the plan" is a vital link in the chain of sanity. Now, before you think there is no spontaneity in our lives, realize that "the plan" is not always set in stone.

Conversation about daily life is essential. When we fail to communicate about the daily activities of the family, we open the door for little disasters that often have "Titanic" consequences. For our family, the day-to-day planning takes place in the living room.

Time management specialists state that beginning your day at work with five solid minutes of organization will save you countless hours over the course of a year. In marital communication, as well, five minutes of planning each day will save numerous arguments and misunderstandings over the course of the day.

On the first working day of each month, we sit down and go over upcoming appointments, games, church meetings, "date nights," and social events. Every Monday morning, we take a few moments to go over our calendars for the week, and every morning we review the "plan" for the day.

Sound too much like the military to you? It did for us, too, until we realized that we enjoyed the freedom this kind of planning brought to our lives. No more double bookings, no more missed appointments, and especially, no more hurt feelings because old blunderhead forgot the date night.

This type of scheduling is critical for our marriage, given our irregular schedules and job responsibilities. For many people whose jobs and schedules are more predictable, it is possible to sit down over a cup of coffee on Saturday morning or Sunday evening and hammer out the week ahead. Either way, "living room" communication about day-to-day events is vital to the smooth operation of any marriage.

The Family Room—
Communication Through Play

We have all heard the cliché, "The family that prays together, stays together." We have another one: "The family that *plays* together, stays together." We are a full contact family. In other words, we show our affection through physical touch. Hugs and kisses, high fives, and pats on the back are all part of the story in our home. One example of our physical nature is when Torrey and I get down and dirty on the floor for some big-time wrestling. I can vividly remember wrestling with my dad, and feel that it is my "responsibility" to pass this "legacy of love on the floor" to my son.

We start out with all the trash talk and walk around each other like Neanderthals. Then, with me on my knees and TJ on my back, we wallow and roll around giving each other fake "supplexes and death grips." Most of the time "wrestle" turns into one giant tickle party, especially now that Grace loves to get into the fray.

What makes this time with the children so special is that it is uninterrupted. It really doesn't matter what activity you and your kids feel comfortable doing; what does matter is that they know you enjoy spending time with just them. The old saying rings true. "People don't care how much you know until they know how much you care."

Remember, "Love is spelled T I M E." As we spend time with our children, we find ways to communicate that are critical to their psychological and emotional development. An open line of communication with your children will become more valuable when the inevitable teenage crisis comes your way, as well as laying the groundwork for them to pursue a positive interpersonal relationship when searching for a spouse.

Playtime is not the only activity in our family room around which conversation revolves. It seems that over the past 20 years television has been viewed as an enemy, a time stealer, a bad influence, and while all of that may be true, there are ways parents can take control and employ its advantages.

The TV has been a vehicle for unwinding in our home. After school, Torrey watches programs of his choice, Dad chooses dramas or sitcoms to relax after a long night on the road, and Mom usually joins the family viewing the program currently in progress. The television initiates conversation in the family room. Torrey prefers to watch reruns of the sitcoms Mom and Dad watched when they were kids. This leads to one of us sharing a childhood experience that may have never been verbalized had we not reviewed that episode of "Gilligan's Island."

Specific scenes on a television program have also been used as a tool for initiating conversation concerning our family values. We screen the shows our children and we as a couple watch, based on the theme of the plot or the language and violence. Discussion precedes many TV shows in our home. All too often time spent in front of the television is regarded as the enemy when, in reality, the content can be used as a tool for learning and spurring discussion with our family.

The Dining Room—
Communication Through the Trivial

Trivial does not mean unimportant! The communication that occurs around our dining room table is simply the rehashing of the events of each person's day.

The Social Hour

As I speak to business leaders around the country, many events include a social hour. During this time, men and women stand around a room chitchatting about topics varying from politics to sports to the latest movie or popular TV show. This small talk allows business associates the time to get to know each other and feel more comfortable by identifying common interests and experiences. Even the best of friends, in business settings, will utilize social occasions as an opportunity to strengthen their relationship. The same principle is true in marriage

Describing the trivial details of the day's events provides your spouse an avenue for understanding your world. It makes her feel a part of your life and becomes an effective means to practice communications skills.

Another tool to foster communication between family members involves discussing current community and national events. Practicing communication skills while making trivial conversation will ultimately produce better skills, particularly when the communication is not so easy. Unfortunately, most of us wait until a serious crisis arises to practice our underdeveloped techniques, which makes reciprocal communication difficult. Remember earlier we discussed how men and women differ in the number of words they speak in a single day. Men speak about 10,000 words in a day, most of them before they get home from work. Women, even if they are employed outside the home, may still have 10,000 more verbal needs to express before bedtime. During the evening meal is a great time for them to complete their allotment of words!

The Kitchen—
Communication Through Serving

"A man may work from sun to sun but a woman's work is never done." All too often in marriage, we forget the most basic rule of empathy. For a moment, put yourself in the other person's shoes. The single best way to accomplish this is through service.

The "little girl" in me loves Christmas! The snow on the ground…the lights decorating the neighborhood…the yummy fragrances that fill our homes…and the gifts…the gifts…THE GIFTS! Honestly, the gifts are my favorite part of Christmas. I love to receive gifts (don't we all), but I really enjoy choosing just the right gift for my friends and family. I enjoy shopping at multiple stores and envisioning the face of each person as they open the gift I've selected.

Jay, on the other hand, is not an organized shopper. Typically, his routine involves waiting until December 24th to purchase my Christmas gift. His explanation is that his perceived procrastination results from experience with my detective skills because I snoop and figure out the contents of the gift box. In my opinion, Jay delays the pain as long as possible. One year, though, the routine was interrupted…

On the first of December Jay strolled into the living room and cautioned me not to peek at the contents of my stocking until Christmas day or the surprise will be ruined. (Yes, our stockings are hung each year by December 1!) His words of wisdom were like placing a ten-pound chunk of Ghirardelli dark chocolate in front of me and telling me not to eat it! I will proudly say, however, that while the contents remained a mystery, I did investigate. The item was a unique gift selection and strangely appeared to be just a piece of paper. On Christmas morning I was rewarded with an amazing surprise!

One part of this story that you need to know is that I am not a house-cleaner. I simply despise housework. Most cleaning duties are palatable but cleaning the bathrooms is the worst possible punishment I can imagine.

On that Christmas morning, I was the proud recipient of the best gift I have ever received! The stocking contents revealed a coupon from Jay promising to clean all the bathrooms for one year! Wow, what a man! Do you know what this gift communicated? "Honey, I understand that you do not like cleaning the bathrooms, and I, your understanding husband, am going to do something about it!" More importantly, I knew that he loved me enough to hear my complaints and take action, and perform an act of service to honor me.

There are various ways to communicate with your spouse through serving Laura and I give each other the freedom to enjoy different endeavors. Each of us selects one a night each week to participate in individual activities without the children and without guilt.

It is important to your personal growth and development to enjoy activities or hobbies that involve interaction with people who share a common interest. Knowing that your spouse is giving you the guilt-free freedom to participate in something that stimulates you mentally, socially, spiritually, or physically is a rewarding form of service that will ultimately benefit your relationship.

The Bedroom—
Communication Through Intimacy

I recall as a small child watching Grandma and Grandpa Laffoon kiss each other goodbye. Grandpa was 6 feet 2 inches tall and nothing but skin and bones. Grandma stood 4 feet 10 inches with her shoes on and was "full figured." It was amusing to watch "Pop" bend his long lanky frame and Grandma rise on her tiptoes as they embraced.

It was also hysterical to note the duration of their kiss. Grandpa was a truck driver and often away from home for days at a time. It made sense that when he was leaving on a trip to Chicago or Detroit that they would embrace to reaffirm their love for each other. But they kissed when Pop was heading to the corner market for bread and milk and would be away from the house for five minutes max—in fact, less time than they spent kissing good-bye! Pop taught me that every kiss a man gives a woman is important. The problem with most of us is that when we leave the house, we have a lot on our minds, resulting in a less-than-desirable effort. I call it the "see-ya" kiss, that short little peck that barely resembles a kiss at all.

I've also learned something about women. In the mind of a woman, kissing is a very intimate deliberate action. This perception is difficult for men to imagine because a kiss doesn't carry the same weight for us. Take a risk; ask your wife if she sees kissing (real kissing) as the most intimate of activities. This is why kissing can be the prelude to our sexual encounters. With this in mind, there is no better way to ensure a great end to the day than to begin the day with a kiss that knocks your wife's socks off. This memory will linger in her mind all day. Then follow this up with a come-home-from-work, passionate "I'm-so-glad-to-see-you" embrace.

Practicing this technique will result in two guaranteed reactions: 1) the first time you do it, she will be suspicious! So don't be surprised if she freaks out, and 2) If you make passionate purposeful kissing a habit, it will most assuredly lead to another habit that you will no doubt fully enjoy at the end of the day.

The Southern Way

Growing up in the "proper South," sex was not something that nice girls talked about among friends, let alone with our husbands! I will be honest and say that intimate communication is and has been the hardest skill for me to learn. One of my college professors introduced the concept that " if a couple can't communicate in the living room, they won't be able to communicate in the bedroom." In reality the reverse is also true because if a couple can't communicate in the bedroom, they won't be able to communicate in any other room of the house. Intimate communication is the most challenging, yet rewarding, communication a couple can share. Multi-level communication is what separates us from the animals! Speaking of animals...

I don't know what happens to a man when he assumes a horizontal position, but something clicks! This is what typically happens in our house; it may sound familiar.

Jay and I complete a full day in the office. The kids are finally in bed sleeping like angels. Tired, we retire to the family room. Sitting together in our chair built for two, we channel surf, watching selected clips of five television shows almost simultaneously. With "power" in hand, Jay guides our attention through the wild wonderful world of global TV! At about 9:00, I notice that the quantity of shows begins to rapidly decrease. And at 9:10, one program has been randomly selected. Jay is asleep. Now in my mind, I am thinking, "Whew, he must really be tired! Poor guy, he must have worked hard today."

The other side of my mind is thinking, "All right! I can go to bed tonight and go right to sleep. Surely, He is too tired to..." I let him sleep in the chair for about an hour. At 10:00, I awaken him so we can proceed upstairs. Still groggy, he drags himself out of the chair and slowly ascends the staircase. The minute we are in bed, however, he suddenly springs to life! What is up? He has slept the evening away, yet the minute his head hits the pillow, he is awake and raring to go! After the short nap, he is no longer too tired to consider alternative activities. My response is, "No way, buddy, that is not how this works!" Needless to say, Jay and I have had volumes of communication about this little scenario!

While that may be a funny scenario, and all too real, Laura and I had to work through it by talking it out, sharing our needs and frustrations. By repeating this pattern in our love life, a monotonous fabric would have been woven. Too often, couples tend to avoid discussing the intimate issues in their lives. While communication about issues surrounding the intimate portion of our relationship, and at times open sharing, may result in painful reality, communication of this depth is vital to a healthy, success-ful bedroom life satisfying to both of you. If either of us had stopped communicating, not shared our feelings, and ignored our God given needs, we would have missed out on some wonderful intimate times in our lives.

The Bathroom—
Communication Through Crisis

Growing up in a small town in Northern Michigan, the Laffoon family lived in a small house with a single solitary small bathroom. Being part of an active family of four, getting ready in the morning or preparing to attend an event as a family was a cooperative effort. Quite honestly, I never really knew what pri-vacy was when it came to occupying the bathroom; it wasn't a common occurrence to have the room all to myself in our little world. I can remember many times when someone would be using the sink while someone else was in the shower while yet another was otherwise occupied.

Presently, as our lifestyle and accommodations have evolved, Mom and Dad share their own bathroom and so do the kids. Laura and I actually enjoy some privacy as we prepare for the day or retire at night. As a result, the bathroom is a place where we can discuss private issues that may be inappropriate for little ears.

When my mother was diagnosed with cancer, Torrey was the only grandchild and adored Grandma Doyce. Laura and I spent numerous hours in the bathroom discussing, weeping, and plan-ning our strategy to handle the situation. Our private hideaway was the perfect place to reach a consensus without upsetting TJ.

In every family, the list of private issues is lengthy including job difficulties, family issues, financial concerns, church problems, social events, or surprise family activities. Whatever the case, there are times when privacy is a must.

Don't get us wrong, we are firm believers in being honest and open about the reality of life's challenges with our children; how-ever, there are proper times and places for such explanations. Mom and Dad need opportunity to process their response to this issue privately. The bathroom may not be your choice for conversations with your spouse, but do find a place where you can converse freely without the intrusion of little ears.

The Car—
Communication Through Vision

A love of travel is either in your blood or it's not. Growing up as the grandson of a truck driver and the son of a youth minister (translation youth trip, youth trip, youth trip), traveling was my destiny. Fortunately, our whole family enjoys nationwide mobility. We are the classic geeky little group tooling along in the family conversion van complete with TV, DVD player, and a hide-a-bed rear compartment. Because I speak in multiple venues each year, having my family accompany me when our schedules coincide is truly a rewarding experience.

I vividly recall the first trip we took in the van to visit Laura's folks in Atlanta for Thanksgiving. Leaving about 6 P.M., we anticipated arriving in Atlanta for breakfast. Cruising along I-75 near Findlay, Ohio, I felt an overwhelming warmth in my heart. Laura asleep on the bed preparing for the next driving shift, Torrey watching the conclusion of a movie before joining Mom in deep slumber, and I was in heaven listening to my collection of 1970's rock 'n' roll. With our course set for Nana's, we all knew our roles and responsibilities for the mission at hand.

Communication about your future is much like a long trip in a car. The first step is planning. Consulting a convenient atlas, you map a course based on the ultimate destination. Second, the role of each family member is identified. Driving non-stop from Alma, Michigan, to Atlanta, Georgia, as a single driver is not a wise decision. Preserving the safe transport of the family warrants a second driver. Torrey, who was four years old at the time, was assigned a single task—to make sure he visited the bathroom during gasoline and meal stops. Not a large responsibility, but a very important part of the plan for a carefree excursion.

In most marriages, one person most often sees the big picture while the other focuses on the details. Jay is the personification of the big picture viewpoint, i.e. the dreamer, the visionary. He envisions fantastic dreams that seem surreal. I, on the other hand, take the big picture concept he's verbalized and draw a map taking into account the necessary steps to achieve the desired goal. If this is what we want to do, then this is how we need to get there. I have learned over the years that we can take any big picture vision the Lord gives Jay and turn it into a reality in our lives.

When traveling in life together, we offer these two simple rules: 1) Know your destination, e.g. where do you want to be financially or spiritually a year from now? and, 2) Define your roles so that each participant has a sense of self-worth and significance and contribution to the outcome. Don't become discouraged when traffic or minor setbacks impede efficient progress toward your goal. Through patience and determination the chosen destination will soon be in view. The Lord has already seen your future and has a wonderful plan that is "beyond all that we ask or think." Remember, He is in control.

We often find ourselves talking about the future when traveling in the car. It could be partially due to daydreaming brought on by the monotony of the white lines or merely habit. Like most of our authentic dreaming, this book was outlined during a return trip from a marriage retreat in Ludington, Michigan.

In conversing about your family's future, you will find yourself dreaming, planning, and growing toward all that God would have you become. Take time to seek a destination towards which God is nudging you. Carefully map out the path required to reach your goal. Perhaps use the time spent together as a couple in the car to converse about your future.

The Basement—
Communication Through Worship

Matthew shares, "Therefore everyone who hears these words of mine and puts them into practice is like a wise man who built his house on the rock. The rain came down, the streams rose, and the winds blew and beat against that house; yet it did not fall, because it had its foundation on the rock" (7:24-25 NIV).

The most important type of communication a person can have is not with their spouse, it's with Jesus. Laying a foundation for communication daily with Christ will enhance and improve communication in every other area of our lives. There is no substitute for being in tune and on track with the Lord.

Building our foundation on a deep personal relationship with the Lord will sharpen and hone every aspect of our being. When our radar is tuned in to the people around us and their individual needs, we begin to see others, especially our spouse, as Jesus sees them. Visualizing our mate with the eyes of Jesus, feeling for them with the heart of Jesus, and especially hearing them with the ears of Jesus will strengthen and enrich our marital bond. With a solid foundation built by daily communication with Christ, we are enabled to intentionally listen to what our spouse needs, instead of just hearing the words spoken in anger or frustration, in joy or exuberance.

When asked to define the difference between listening and hearing, a 12-year-old boy answered, "Listening is wanting to hear."

Communication manifests itself on many levels in a marriage relationship._Sometimes relating to one another is easy and other times it is extremely difficult to understand a conflicting point of view. All forms of communication can be rewarding, however. Communication is the key to celebrating your marriage throughout a lifetime and it can be done in every room of your house.

Why not...

+ You and your spouse rate yourself on a scale 1-10 in each of the areas of communication. Now exchange papers and get a "grade" on how accurate you were.

+ Pick the top way you and your spouse communicate, and ask yourself why that area seems to be easier than others.

+ Take an area that really needs help and ask each other what actions need to be taken to start improvement.

Four

You Gotta
Learn

*E*very June, Laura and I have the privilege of directing a camp in Colorado for two weeks. It is a wonderful experience, and part of the fun is to watch speakers and musicians from various parts of the country as they interact with teens. One memorable speaker was Tim Atkins. Tim was "Jim Carey" before Jim Carey. He is a professional goofball with a heart for kids as big as the Rocky Mountains.

The year Tim spoke, I noticed a unique occurrence very early in the week. No matter where Tim went, he was surrounded by a group of kids. I thought maybe he had groupies from another camp where he had spoken, but then I realized the group of teenagers varied frequently throughout the day.

The next day on the rappelling hill as Tim and some kids were waiting their turn, I discovered his secret. He was playing a game he's dubbed "Trivia." Tim starts by letting a student choose the topic. Alex cries out "Geography!" Without hesitation, Tim will pose a question such as, "Who are the four figures carved on the face of Mount Rushmore?" When Andrea answers correctly, Tim acknowledges her and repeats "topic." Andrea responds "Sports" and Tim fires back, "What team won the 1979 NCAA men's division I basketball tournament." Mike shouts "Michigan State!" and the process continues.

Tim maintained this challenge of wit for over 30 to 40 minutes at a time, firing one question after another addressing any and every topic the kids could propose. Amazed, I asked him, "How do you do that?" Tim's answer and its truth are unforgettable. "Jay, life is cumulative. If I don't know more today than I did yesterday, then I've wasted a chance to learn. I'm fortunate to be able to remember what I learn."

Life is cumulative—marriage is cumulative! Each one of us can build a marriage that is vibrant and growing, by developing the following five characteristics that will help us learn to celebrate!

Dream

If you could design a dream marriage, a dream lifestyle, what would it look like? Are you so bogged down in the day-to-day routine that to dream anything seems too hard to imagine? Laura and I had a dream to speak and work together helping marriages, families, and teens grow, mature, and become all God intended them to be. We also had a dream of one day writing a book, but that seemed like such a long time ago.

As an avid reader, I followed in my mother's footsteps. She has made reading a priority for as long as I can remember. My earliest recollections involve hiding a flashlight under my bed so at bedtime I could close the door, turn out the light, hide under the covers, and read until I fell asleep, aspiring one day to become a great author. Among my favorite books are historical novels in which the facts of American history are entwined with fiction—just the kind of book I dreamed of writing,

In college, I planned to major in English and minor in journalism, but I was soon challenged by a new dream—ministry. Choosing a major of social ministries, the dream of writing a book became less a priority. Until I met Jay, my dream lay dormant, having never been shared with anyone else.

Jay is the unfailing "Mr. Encouragement" and he wanted to see me fulfill my dream. However, our lives were soon filled with two children, a full time ministry, teens knocking at our door day and night…therefore, having the time or the energy to pen a manuscript seemed a remote possibility.

But Jay would never allow my dream to drift too far away. "One day we are going to write a book," he would enthusiastically announce. Over the past six years, we have traveled across the country challenging couples at marriage retreats, and with each bit of research and all the preparation of presentation materials, completing the book began to become a reality. "We should write a book," Jay would say. "You can write a book," I would reply. As a speaker, he has quite a way with words, and I was sure that my dream should really be his dream. But "Mr. Encouragement" never gives up so here it is—my dream fulfilled 30 years later!

Dreams are important to our future, for they encourage us and give us something for which to strive. What are your dreams for today? For tomorrow? What do you want to be doing in ten years? How do you want your marriage relationship to grow over the next ten years?

Dream!

Trust

A trust fall is when your faith is exercised by a person standing on a table and falling face up into a group, trusting total strangers to intervene before gravity wins. This group activity can be a wonderful tool to build a sense of community.

Scott Davis has put a bit of a twist on the old trust fall. My friend secures a 10 to 12 foot stepladder. He then selects a very large man from the audience and instructs the man to climb to the first step. With the man facing the ladder, Scott asks him to fall backwards into his arms. Ninety-nine times out of a hundred, the chosen one will cooperate and Scott will share a few moments on the value of trust.

Scott then asks the man to climb to the top of the ladder. Summoning a petite woman out of the audience he shares that this man will now fall from eight feet into the arms of this woman, and 99 times out of 100 the man says, "No way!" You can imagine the chuckles Scott gets from the audience as he ribs the man about what little faith he has in this woman. And you can imagine the woman's relief when she realizes she won't have to attempt to catch this big bruiser. In the one instance when the man says okay and attempts to fall, Scott steps in before the man completes the fall and the woman's color returns.

In summary, Scott inquires about the size of our trust. He says, "It's not so much how far you're going to fall, it's how much faith you have in the one who will catch you. The reason most people don't trust is because their perspective of God is exceptionally small. They do not realize how great and mighty is the Lord who loves them. Whether we want to admit it or not, we become indoctrinated with the image of a 'Sunday school Jesus' who walked around on a flannelgraph, rather than the Lord of life who merely spoke and the universe came into being."

How high is your level of trust? We must learn to build our trust every day with our Lord and our spouse. Building trust is like taking a sheet of paper once a day and placing it on a pile. As we add a sheet each day, the pile doesn't appear to grow. But come back in a year and you will behold a large fortress of paper.

In a similar way, we build trust with our spouse. Each day we learn to trust them a little more. Though subtle, the change from day to day is building and growing, and a year from now, if the trust is not broken, we will note a tremendous difference.

Realizing that we need to trust our spouse, how do we construct that pile each day, especially if they have done something to disturb the foundation of trust? There are five ways:

1) **T**rust Jesus. The only person you can trust without question is Jesus. You must place your trust in the Holy and Almighty God and allow Him to have control of your life.

2) **R**ecognize that your spouse is going to let you down. The most unfair thing we can do to our spouse is to expect eternal

perfection. We all are human and make mistakes. Standing on top of a pedestal is not a comfortable place. It is a long fall to the bottom. Setting unrealistic expectations for your spouse will only lead to heartache and frustration in your marriage.

3) **U**nderstand the forgiveness factor. Trust cannot be rebuilt until forgiveness occurs. True forgiveness is accepting your spouse's apology and moving on. Forget about the mistake and wipe the slate clean. That is what Jesus does for us! Though this step may be difficult, with God's help you will be able to deal with your spouse's shortcomings and move on.

4) **S**peak your trust. The above three steps all happen on the inside. Now let your spouse hear that you trust him or her. Until we verbalize the things in our hearts and minds, they don't become real. Express your trust to your spouse in words.

5) **T**rust. Now for the action scene. Real trust initiates follow-through. Once you realize your spouse will never attain perfection and you have forgiven anything that has robbed the mutual trust you shared, and verbalized to your spouse that you trust him or her, you must put it into action. Trust.

Trust is a learning process. Through a perpetual process we must learn how to trust Jesus and how to trust our spouse. Trusting our chosen partner is a vital part of celebrating our marriage.

Conflict

The first fight Jay and I ever had was over a sleeve of Oreo cookies! Engaged for about two months, we attended Bill and Gloria Gaither's Praise Gathering conference with Jay's family in Indianapolis, Indiana. After a long and tiring day, Jay, his sister Diane, and I decided to remain at the hotel for the evening. I had a taste for Oreos and Jay, being a wonderful fiancé, trudged down to the hotel gift shop. What a man! He returned empty-handed. "The Oreos were too expensive," he said, "and I was not going to pay $3.52 for eight cookies!" Exhausted and famished, I stomped out of the suite and stowed away to my bedroom What kind of man was I marrying? He didn't care enough about me to buy me cookies! What an inconsiderate slob, what a cheapskate, what a...

I can't remember who initiated the resolution, Jay or me, but we did resolve the conflict as we both understood the 100-year principle: "If it's not going to matter in 100 years, then it's probably not worth fighting about." We learned a few things about each other that day, namely, he is too tight with the buck and I am spoiled! You may laugh, but it is true! We learned, too, that conflict teaches us volumes. These lessons have followed us throughout our married life. We have learned how to fight fair, resolve our differences, and enjoy making up. Conflict is learning. Conflict is necessary.

Communication

The story is told of a naval captain aboard a destroyer. This captain had a decorated naval career and rose through the ranks to command the very large crew on this ship.

One morning the air was filled with fog, and the crew was tense as they slipped through the icy waters. Ahead in the distance, a spotter on the bridge noticed a light that appeared to be another ship on a direct collision course with the destroyer. Without delay the captain ordered his radio operator to send word to the other ship, "We are on a collision course. Please change your heading." A simple message returned, "You change your heading."

The captain was annoyed and fired back "This is Captain J.J. Johnson of the U.S. navy. Enough foolishness, now change your heading." The message came back. "This is Ensign First Class S.D. Martin; you must change your course."

By now the captain was furious; this ensign was about to push this grizzled veteran too far. "I am the captain of a large destroyer. Now move or be struck!" The return message was simple and clear: "Captain, I'm in a lighthouse." Without delay, the enormous destroyer changed its course.

Does that little exchange remind you of anything? All too often, our marital communication seems to be delivered in short unclear messages engulfed in the fog of day-to-day activity. We banter back and forth, back and forth, never clearly seeing the obvious solution right in front of us. Learning to communicate on a consistent basis with love and care should be our goal. It doesn't happen overnight, however. In order to achieve effective communication, we must continually practice our listening skills.

Don't you just hate it when you are pouring out your heart to someone and you realize he or she hasn't heard a word you've said? At times, we all feel as though we've been talking to a brick wall.

Practicing empathy for another person fosters a new perspective, the same as walking a mile in someone else's shoes. One classic experiment I think every married couple should experience, if possible, concerns empathy. Pick a day, any day. On that day the wife should live the husband's life and the husband should live the wife's life. If he works, she should go to the job site, complete his shift, and deal with his boss, clients, and coworkers. If the wife works outside the home, he should fulfill her responsibilities for that day. If she doesn't work outside the home, he stays home, transports the kids to school and to their various other activities, cleans the house, prepares dinner, and so on. I think a single day's walk in our spouse's shoes would enhance our understanding of life from their perspective.

Listening and empathy are the foundational blocks upon which effective communication is built.

Worship

> *"Therefore, I urge you brethren, by the mercies of God to present your bodies as living sacrifices, holy and acceptable to God. This is your spiritual worship. Do not be conformed to this world, but be transformed by the renewing of your mind, that you may prove what the will of God is. His good and perfect will"* (Romans 12:1-2).

God wants my body? No way! Has God seen me naked in front of the mirror lately? That fine physique my wife married has changed a bit...okay, a lot. Why would God want my body? Our bodies are the primary vehicle we can use to demonstrate our love for Him. It's also the primary way we show our spouse we love them. In a word, sacrifice, or as Paul describes, a *living* sacrifice.

The main problem with a living sacrifice is that it keeps crawling off the altar over and over again. The same is true in marriage. We long in the early years to sacrifice luxuries for the good of our marriage. Men will give up watching a ballgame to take a walk with their wife and have a long conversation. Similarly, women will act as if they really enjoy sports, just to spend time with their husbands. In any case, we offered our bodies up to each other in various ways; however, as time passes, the sacrificial attitude wanes in the everyday humdrum, resulting in the sacrifice crawling off the altar.

What is the ultimate "offering" of our bodies? The ultimate sacrifice? The ultimate sacrifice happens to be the ultimate form of worship, that's right, worship.

One of my favorite professors in college was Sig Zielke. I liked Sig for a number of reasons, he was "cool" and would listen and counsel with students. But the deepest impression was made by his passionate and intriguing mode of teaching. One day I listened to what I thought was the best news I'd ever heard. Sig noted that the ultimate form of worship occurred when a Christian husband and wife made love. Of course everyone's hormone-filled ears perked up. Sig's message was simple: Worship is offering our bodies to God, and reflecting His power, majesty, and love. What a picture was expressed in those few words. Great news to my ears but a strange concept to grasp.

Without getting too graphic, when a believing husband and wife offer their bodies to each other in total abandon, and Christ is at the center of that marriage, it is a perfect reflection (worship) of the Triune God (three in one). This bond of husband, wife, and Christ is meant to be a place of worship and adoration of our maker. Simply put, a slice of heaven on earth. Unfortunately, the world and our perverted minds have taken this highest form of worship and twisted it into something, that doesn't even resemble its original purpose.

We must support our local churches, worship corporately and be inspired, but there is no higher form of worship than when a husband and wife give wholeheartedly to each other, offering their best without expecting anything in return. We must learn to worship at the altar of the marriage bed and keep it holy for it is ordained and consecrated by God.

Why not...

+ Share with your spouse your dreams...for today, this year, your marriage.
+ List the different ways your spouse builds trust with you.
+ Recall the last conflict you had and ask how it could have been avoided.
+ Worship together in a unique way this week.

Five

You Gotta
Labor

I am an exercise nut! I enjoy all forms of exercise. One favorite exercise is to simply pull on my running shoes and accept the challenge of the external environment. Winter in Michigan is a little slushy, so a few years ago, we joined the local fitness center at Alma College and at noon everyday, Jay and I would run. The noontime hour was advantageous due to fewer college students using the fitness equipment and because friends would join us to share the agony of exercise.

I recall one time when I ventured into the fitness center and life became hard. As I sat on the exercise mat to put on my shoes, I noted a young coed on the mat next to mine. Here I was struggling to stretch far enough to lace up my shoes and she was doing an abdominal workout at a rate of 100 crunches per second! Thus began my longing to be 21 again!

After putting on the shoes, came the long walk to the treadmill. I stepped on and punched in the numbers to begin a slow stretch walk and *then the gradual acceleration to "the run." The young coed appeared on the adjacent treadmill, running at the same breakneck pace at which she performed the ab workout! "Okay Laura, look out the window and think of something else. You will never be 21 again!"*

It is amazing when we take our eyes off of ourselves, how the Lord teaches us. While pondering the treadmill, I discovered that one reason running outside is rewarding involves the sense of accomplishment when I reach the destination. On the treadmill, you can run and run and sweat and sweat and when it is all over...you are still right where you started, looking at the same scenery. The challenges of life draw a similar parallel. We can climb on and do all the right things, work really hard, volunteer in worthy endeavors, attend church, take care of our family, spend time with our friends, and even love our spouse, yet feel as though we're going nowhere!

In this chapter, we are going to discuss how to step off the treadmill and progress to your destination.

Jay was conducting a teamwork seminar for a local group of dentists. He had spent the day dealing with issues like stress in the workplace and the different hats that we all wear in our daily activities. The goal for the day was to move the group toward thinking about the mission or purpose of their particular dentistry practice.

After posing the question, "What is the significance of June 6,1944?", a blanket of silence covered the room, indicating a degree of discomfort. People began to whisper back and forth, thinking out loud. They knew the date had something to do with World War II, but what was the significance? Frank sat in the back of the room. Though he pioneered this particular dental practice a number of years ago, he remained physically fit for a semi-retired man in his 70s, only frequenting the office a couple of days a week. He cleared his voice, and with a confidence found only in one who had been there, replied, "D-day."

"Correct," Jay responded. There was a brief sigh of relief as tension exited the room.

Then Jay fired back, "What was the mission of D-day?" This time many in the room felt the freedom to express their opinion of the true mission of that particular military exercise. Most were filled with lofty words about the American way or the atrocities of the Nazis under

Hitler. All true, but none quite caught the mission. Again, as Frank cleared his voice, the room sat in a silent tribute to his wisdom and knowledge. "Free Europe" was his firm response. Immediately every one in the room understood what each man who stormed the beaches of Normandy understood. Everything they did, everything they were about to sacrifice, every casualty was weighed against the mission to "Free Europe."

If we were to ask you the mission of your marriage or family, could you or your spouse or your children clearly articulate it?

In 1973 a study during the Kennedy Administration concluded that America had shifted its focus from the family to the workplace. JFK's words, "Ask not what your country can do for you, ask what you can do for your country," gave people the inspiration to make something of their lives. In the aftermath lay the broken and shattered families that we deal with today.

Every couple can develop a family Mission Statement by following the four steps outlined below.

Step #1. *Determine Your Core Values*

What matters to you? What matters to your spouse? Your kids? Core Values are simply those people, activities, beliefs, or things that matter most, ranging from concepts like love and acceptance, to something material like a house. Core Values are different for every person.

Some would say that only concepts can be values. We have experienced, however, that values are often expressed by the activities in which we participate or the feelings that a particular place or object might generate within us.

For example, Laura grew up in Atlanta, Georgia, a major metropolitan area where anything and everything is easily accessible. I grew up in Petoskey, Michigan, a classic small midwestern town. For the first three years of our marriage we lived in Atlanta. Laura thought life was wonderful, but I was less comfortable living in the metropolitan jungle.

It was Laura who suggested we pursue moving to Michigan. It was Laura who first thought that Alma was the town for us. It is now Laura who wouldn't leave Alma for anything in the world. Her Core Values now include the benefits of small town living. Thus, places and things—while they may not be values in concept—do generate within us feelings and emotions that can be categorized as values.

The first step in developing a Family Mission Statement is to list your Core Values. Now, don't sit down one night at the dinner table and try to think of everything that is important to you. It's simply not possible.

Start with a manila envelope or file folder. Keep it accessible and in plain sight. Each day write down one Core Value, and place it in the envelope. Sometimes a Core Value will become evident while you're driving to work or the store, or enter your conscious reality through the verse of song or a line in a poem. Discussion of an issue over a meal or date may identify a Core Value. Please don't rush the process; allow 30 to 60 days to generate as many values as you can.

Now take a Saturday morning, a Sunday evening, or whenever is convenient and dump all the Core Values you have written on a table. Categorize them by topic or any logical category that makes sense to you.

If you don't understand a particular value that your spouse has written, take the time to have her explain it to you. It may be a value you already share. For example, one value that Laura identified was "fun." I didn't completely grasp the meaning until she explained that it was important for her to be stimulated by experiences we would share. Suddenly what Laura had written made perfect sense.

Pay particular attention to Core Values that you both wrote down. They will be a great bridge to build on in step #2.

Step #2. *Discover Your Central Core Value*

In youth ministry, we played a game with the teens that went along with the focus that night of "priorities." It was a fun game, and gave us some deep insight into what really mattered to them.

We passed out pads and pencils and asked them to list the ten most important things in their life, explaining that "things" could mean anything from people to ideas to material possessions—anything they felt they couldn't live without.

We strongly encouraged the kids to make choices based on their true feelings and beliefs, explaining that the root of the word *belief* means "to live by." Their decisions should be based on what they were prepared to live by, not just what they thought sounded impressive.

Next we told them to choose two they would give up, decreasing their list to eight items. For some, choosing was easy; for others it was a little more painful and time consuming.

The process was repeated, paring their list down to six, then four, then two, then one. We wanted to find out what was of highest importance in these kids' lives.

The discussion which followed was prodded by the question, "Tell us why you chose to leave behind what you did and why you kept what you did?"

Forever ingrained in my memory are the words, "Why can't you be more like your sister?" I am sure many of you share a similar memory. My persistent retort echoed, "Because I am not my sister, I am me!" As a result, one of my central Core Values is to be unique. Whatever I do, how I decorate my house, how I dress, how I live my life, I want to be unique. I want to be me!

Hopefully, you're already a step ahead of us. Write down your top ten Core Values as a couple or a family.

Now comes the process of discovering your Central Core Value. The way to do this is through open discussion, asking each other which of these values you could live without if you absolutely had to. Start by paring your list down to eight, then six, and so on until you identify (through mutual consent and support) that single Core Value around which you will build your lives.

This process may be intense. For some the paring process could take weeks or months of discussion, prayer, and soul searching. For others, it may not be that difficult, as you discover that even though you may express it in different terms, you and your spouse are on the same page when it comes to your Core Values.

It's truly a distillation process. A number of years ago, my parents began to suffer from arthritis. Grandma Doyce had joint stiffness so bad in her hands that she couldn't pick up a carton of milk without pain. Poppa Jim experienced constant pain in his hip from an old skiing accident. They began to research non-pharmaceutical methods to alleviate the pain and discovered reliable evidence that drinking distilled water could provide some relief. It sounds too simple to be effective, but since investing in a water distiller and exclusively using distilled drinking water (coffee, tea, ice cubes, juice concentrates, etc.), their symptoms of arthritis have subsided. The reason is that the distillation process removes all the contaminates, it boils, filters, and eliminates impurities. Is it easy to distill four gallons of water a day? No. Is it necessary? Yes, if they want to live pain-free lives.

Now, we are not about to say that discovering your Central Core Value will eliminate pain from your marriage or family. It will, however, provide a basis for celebration, direction, and joy. After discovering that Central Core Value, you will be ready for the third step.

Step #3. *Devise Your Family Mission Statement*

Growing up, we all have our favorite subjects in school and those we could definitely live without. For me, geometry proposed too many formulas for my mind to grasp, and though Mr. Swenor was a likeable teacher, the subject content fell on deaf ears.

To successfully devise your Family Mission Statement, we recommend a formula. It is not the *end all, be all*, but it does provide a solid foundation for you and your family to build a mission statement that is poignant, pregnant, and bursting forth with truths to live by.

First, review the Core Values on your top ten list and find the final three to five. These additional Core Values are what we call Subsequent Core Values. They are not your Central Core Value, but are of extremely high importance to you. If you examine them closely, they may support or parallel the achievement of your Central Core Value.

Following is the Laffoon Family Mission Statement that you can use as a sample.

Our Family Mission
To encourage others to become like Christ through loving relationships, healthy lifestyles, and stimulating experiences.

The formula is quite simple and reads as follows: To (insert Central Core Value here) by [or through] (insert three to five Subsequent Core Values here). Sounds too simple, doesn't it? Formulas can't be that easy—or can they?

Let's look at our Mission Statement again. Our Central Core Value was *encouraging others to become like Christ.* This surpassed our immediate family to include the people that we encounter in Alma every day, and through many speaking and workshop settings across the country. We accomplish this through our Subsequent Core Values of *loving relationships* (with our family and friends), *healthy lifestyles* (balancing all areas of life), and *stimulating experiences* (a phrase which encompasses Laura's idea of "fun").

In the space below, fill in the words of the Central Core Value you've identified and any Subsequent Core Values which support it. After writing it, say it out loud and see if the words ring true in your heart and mind. We've seen this process produce believable results and we hope you'll find this too.

To_____,
Through _____
_____
_____.

Developing a Family Mission Statement will help you step off the treadmill and begin to move in the direction the Lord has given you. Focusing on the values you hold dear in your life will help you stay on course and not allow you to stray back to the treadmill.

After Jay and I completed this process, I had to evaluate my activities and decide whether they were keeping me on the treadmill or facilitating the accomplishment of my mission. While they were all worthy causes, I now had the freedom to say "no."

The fun is about to begin! Ready for step 4?

Step #4. Develop Positive Personal Habits

We will discuss how to change our habits in chapter 6, but suffice to say each one of us is 100 percent disciplined to the habits that we practice. That's right, 100 percent as disciplined as we will ever be. We're 100 percent disciplined to the good habits in our life and 100 percent disciplined to the bad habits in our life. That's depressing! The key is to develop positive personal habits to live by.

Some people call them rules, and while it may only be semantics, people don't like rules. Most of us see a list of rules, turn our back, and run because we know we can never live up to the standard of perfection we have set for ourselves.

We believe that no one is perfect and as a result, we challenge people to focus on progress, not perfection. It is amazing what this small paradigm shift can accomplish. As people focus on their progress toward positive habits, they feel a sense of accomplishment and success rather than imperfection and failure. So, while the following may look like rules of the house, trust us, they are *habits* of the house.

Your final step in the Family Mission Statement process is to give you and your family a framework in which to live out your mission. Again, this may seem too simple, but the best way is to review the Core Values your family recorded in the file folder. These can ultimately be expressed as habits you and your spouse or family desire to practice. Here are the Laffoons' 25 Habits of the House:

Habits of Our House
We obey the Lord Jesus Christ.

We love, honor, and pray for each other.

We tell the truth.

We consider one another's interest ahead of our own.

We do not hurt each other with unkind words or deeds.

We speak quietly and respectfully to one another.

When someone is sorry, we forgive him.

When someone is happy, we rejoice with him.

When someone is sad, we comfort him.

When someone needs correction, we correct him in love.

When we have something nice to share, we share it.

We take good care of everything God has given us.

We do not create unnecessary work for others.

When we have work to do, we do it without complaining.

When we open something, we close it.

When we turn something on, we turn it off.

When we don't know what to do, we ask.

When we take something out, we put it away.

When we make a mess, we clean it up.

We arrive on time.

We do what we say.

We finish what we start.

We say please and thank you.

When we go out, we act as if we are in this house.

When necessary, we accept discipline and instruction.

Now you possess power and freedom you may have never experienced before. The reality is that these documents—both the Family Mission Statement, and the Habits of the House—are "Living Documents." They are not etched on tablets of stone and may need to be reviewed and revised from time to time, but they do provide guidelines to build a home filled with celebration.

Why not...

✦ Start the Family Mission Statement process today.

✦ Begin by writing down some values, and putting the list in a common place where you and your spouse will see it daily.

✦ Discuss what your values are and the values you both share.

Six

You Gotta
Live

*W*hen Torrey was three years old, he discovered life beyond Barney. I'm not exactly sure how, but until this time, Laura and I had convinced Torrey that all TV had to offer was found on PBS. We had fed him a steady diet of Sesame Street, Lambchop's Playhouse, and that big lovable purple dinosaur. However, TJ (Torrey James) soon discovered the world of cartoons. At 32, I hadn't watched cartoons since I was...I don't know...28 or 29. Boy, had they changed! Laura and I decided we were going to have to censor—that's right, censor—the cartoons our son was going to watch.

I came home early from work one afternoon, and TJ asked if he could watch TV. Entering the family room, I flicked on the tube. While I was surfing through the channels, speeding toward WCMU, the local PBS affiliate, TJ screamed, "Stop, Daddy." Kid commercials blared a familiar jingle promoting sugar-coated cereals, fruity snacks, and the latest action hero toy. Torrey informed me that this was the station he preferred to watch so I endured the commercial barrage to evaluate the ensuing program.

As soon as the "Beetlejuice" intro flashed on the screen, I flicked to the next station. Now, if you are a card carrying member of your local Beetlejuice fan club, then please accept my apologies; however, I was not going to let my three-year-old watch a show about a demon named after Satan himself.

Before I could offer an explanation, Torrey yelled, "DAAADY, I want to watch that show." "No way!" Was all I could say. We proceeded to argue, not just discuss, mind you, but argue for the next three minutes. It was like watching a vicious Doberman pinscher and a ferocious miniature poodle barking at each other and straining against the ends of their leashes—my three-year-old son in a red-faced "take that!" kind of an argument with his 32-year-old-executive-trained-to-work-with-teenagers-dad.

In a moment of parental brilliance (which will only reoccur at the next sighting of Halley's Comet) an idea sparked electrons in my brain. Our family had been studying Charles Sheldon's masterpiece entitled "In His Steps." It had been rewritten for children, and it had become a part of our daily devotions. The premise of the book is to ask yourself the question—no matter who you are, no matter where you are, no matter what the situation—"What would Jesus do?"

I asked TJ, "Buddy, do you remember what we are reading in the morning?"

"Yes, Daddy, it's the 'What Would Jesus Do?' book."

"And son, do you remember what we're supposed to ask?"

"Yes sir, we ask 'What would Jesus do?' "

"That's right, so I'm going to let you watch Beetlejuice."

"Oh Daddy!" he squealed as he wrapped his arms around my leg. "You're the greatest!!!"

"TJ, I want you to do me a favor. I want you to play pretend while you watch TV." His eyes lit up. Pretend was his absolute favorite game in the world.

"I want you to sit over here while you watch the show." I pointed him to a double chair in our family room. (It's not a love seat; it's a double chair with an ottoman where his mom and I *cuddle* while we watch TV.)

"OK Daddy, what do you want me to pretend?"

"Well, I want you to pretend that Jesus is sitting in the chair next to you, watching Beetlejuice with you."

His eyes grew large with the thought. "You mean Jesus could sit right here?" He pointed to the empty space beside him.

"Yes, of course," I said, "and I want you to ask Jesus if He would watch the show. Okay?"

"OOOOKaayyyy!"

"Now, I'm going into the living room and after a while, you ask Jesus if He would watch Beetlejuice, and tell me what He says."

"Okeydokey, Daddy!"

I wasn't in the living room three minutes when in comes TJ, walking slowly, head down, body shifting back and forth as he shuffled along. He moved in very close without saying a word, then he sighed a couple of times. (Inside, I was exploding with anticipation.) "Daddy," he said without moving his lips. (I have found there are two types of people who can talk without moving their lips...little kids and wives when they're really mad!) "Daddy—" one more sigh—"Jesus wouldn't watch Beetlejuice."

(Okay, Jay, stay calm...don't let him know you're jumping for joy on the inside.) "Hmmmm," I gave him that parental nod. "I thought so, son. Would you like to watch something else?"

"Yes sir, how about Lambchop...?"

"OK!"

Later that night, Laura and I were in "the chair," and I recounted what a wonderful dad I had been that day. She nodded with that, "Yeah, yeah, yeah...like your ego needs any more strokes" kind of response. It was around 10 o'clock, and I was almost asleep. (Men, you need to understand that women know when we're almost asleep while watching TV. The channel surfing loses momentum and the remote control stops clicking so fast.) Anyway, I was fading, and Laura knew she had to find something before I lost consciousness. We came across the show "Baywatch." I, to this day, do not know why my wife likes this show but she does. Frankly, I was not about to argue. Mysteriously, I was suddenly not so tired after all. There it was, "Baywatch," exploding with *all* that it has to offer right in front of my eyes. I was minding my own business, thoroughly enjoying all the benefits cable TV has to offer, when this little voice spoke up in the back of my brain. It was Torrey…and guess what he was saying…

"Daddy, would Jesus watch 'Baywatch'?" I dismissed the voice as indigestion or something. Then again, only louder, "Daddy, would Jesus watch 'Baywatch'?" I literally turned my head and said, "Shut up!" Laura looked at me like I was losing it. I smiled, shrugged, and blankly stared at the television.

At this point I could no longer hear anything but Torrey in my head asking the obvious question. Now, if you are the president of the local "Baywatch" fan club, don't get me wrong. Know that I have nothing against David Hasselbutt or Pamela Sue Anderboob. I just knew that the thoughts and images that this show was putting into my head and my heart did not and would not honor my Lord or my wife.

I turned to Laura and explained my dilemma.

She understood.

I'm pretty sure it's a gift, but she always, always understands.

Maybe that's why I feel my life is so full. I live with a woman who understands me, even when I humbly confess my weaknesses as a human being. Laura makes my life feel complete. I believe one of the ways Christ gives us "abundant life" is through the blessings of the people around us—in particular, our spouse. While Jesus is the source of abundant life, I believe He channels his love and grace through the many people in our lives. This leads me to this question:

Are you full or empty? Wouldn't it be great if every day we could be privy to a little gas gauge on the forehead of those around us that would let us know if they were full or empty? Life would be so much easier to handle, because we would know why our spouse yelled at us or why the man at the hardware store was so grumpy. In many ways, however, it's fortunate that we don't have this gauge as I think far too many of us run dangerously close to empty the majority of the time.

Jesus said "I have come that you might have life, and have it to the full" (John 10:10). Every time I read that statement, I ponder the thought of being "full" all the time. There are times, and thankfully so, when I feel completely full. I am blessed to be living the life Christ has for me, with a wife and two children I absolutely adore. I'm blessed with a job I love, and live in a town with people I like. Trust me when I tell you that I count my blessings daily.

There are times, however, when I feel empty. Most often it is the result of my own actions. I go too fast, spend too little time with the Lord, neglect family and friends, and find myself running on fumes. How do we maintain a full life and keep our life tank from running on empty? The twelfth chapter of Romans, verses one and two, offer a solution. Every married couple can find abundant life by implementing the truths found in Paul's letter to the Romans.

> *Therefore, I urge you, brothers, in view of God's mercy, to offer your bodies as living sacrifices, holy and pleasing to God—which is your spiritual worship. Do not conform any longer to the pattern of this world, but be transformed by the renewing of your mind. Then you will be able to test and approve what God's will is—his good, pleasing and perfect will.* (Romans 12:1-2 NIV)

I always like to start with the end in mind, so what is the end, or goal, of this verse? It is to test and approve what God's will is, not just His will, but His good will, His pleasing will, His perfect will. Now to me, if we discover God's will, then there is no way we can be anything but full.

Transform Your Thinking

Working back from our goal, the first truth we must embrace is that we must "transform our mind." That's pretty hard for most of us to do. Our minds get into grooves, thought patterns—okay, let's call them what they are…ruts—and we can't get out of them.

Steven Covey calls this transformation a "paradigm shift." In his book *The Seven Habits of Highly Effective People*, Covey records the history of the Swiss and their wonderful ability to make watches.

For decades, the Swiss were known to make the finest watches in the world. At one point, 90 percent of all watches in the world were made in Switzerland. Then the Swiss made a crucial error. A research and development team in one of their factories invented a new way to run a watch called quartz timing. Up until this point, watches were wound and the tiny little gears and mechanisms inside were what made Swiss watches stand apart from other watches. The proud Swiss found the new technology to be inferior, not up to their high standards and tolerances so, after a period of time, they let the patent run out.

Enter the Japanese, who took the quartz technology and began to work with it. The first watches they produced were also inferior, causing the Swiss to stand by with smug looks on their faces and an "I told you so" attitude. But the Japanese kept working, kept improving. They did not believe the old paradigm that the best watches had to have gears and mechanisms. Slowly, this new paradigm began to pay off. The Japanese improved the quality, durability, and function of the quartz watch, and today, when most people look to their wrist for the correct time, they look at a quartz-operating timepiece.

The Swiss? They now make about 10 percent of the watches in the world. It is amazing what a paradigm shift will do when you take the time to play it out.

This is exactly what the apostle Paul is conveying when he asserts we must transform our minds. We must put away our old ways of thinking about what constitutes a solid marriage and seek from the Lord new and challenging thoughts about His will. His good, pleasing, and perfect will.

Henry Ford said, "Thinking is the hardest work a man can do. That's why so few of us do it." How true! It takes genuine effort, time, and energy to change the way we think. This is the first truth we must embrace if we are going to live life to the fullest.

I enjoy watching magic tricks. My amusement stems from an experience I had as an eight-year-old boy with a magician friend who asked me to assist him with a magic show. I will never forget how I felt as I watched the children in the audience utterly amazed by the tricks I knew were quite simple. Most magic is rather simple: a distraction, a minor change in reality, or slight of hand. What really takes place is that someone thought through the idea of doing something differently.

Dave, "Sparky," is just a regular guy who resides in Alma with his wife Toni and four children. Toni and Laura are in a woman's Bible study from our church. Recently, these ladies embarked on a "women's weekend away," while the guys agreed to stay at home and care for the kids. On the Sunday before the big weekend, Dave came to me and said, "Why don't we send a dozen roses to the condo where the girls are staying, with a note saying 'Have a great time. Love, the guys.'" I said, "I'm all for it, Sparky! Let's do it!"

You see, it only took a little thought on Dave's part to take an idea and watch it blossom into an action that built life into every one of the marriages involved. Is there any question why I've dubbed him "Sparky"?

So how do we transform our thinking? Well, it's an interesting process. My son is an expert on transformers, those little toys that look like a spaceship or a truck. After moving specific components, presto, you've got a robot or an animal or another totally different toy.

What I find interesting about transformers is that even though the toy looks totally different from when you started, all of the parts stay the same. The same is true about transformed minds. You see, Christ takes us where we are and simply rearranges our perspective on life. He performs the transformation when we begin to realize the truth of this passage of scripture: "Since, then, you have been raised with Christ, set your hearts on things above, where Christ is seated at the right hand of God. Set your minds on things above, not on earthly things." (Colossians 3:1-2 NIV).

The transformation that takes place is supernatural. Christ transforms the way we look at life, our spouse, and the life we have together.

Conform Your Will

"Do not conform any longer to the pattern of this world." We are such a conformist country. We speak highly of our uniqueness, but deep inside we all reflect the characteristics common to our peer group. The same is true in Christianity. Instead of believing that God is big enough to give us our own unique ministry, we buy up every book on the market and copy every successful ministry trying to manufacture a ministry which is merely a shadow of what the Lord is doing someplace else. Our marriages deserve more!

God has a unique and wonderful plan for marriage. This book is not meant to be a manual for fashioning your marriage to look like ours. Rather, it is meant to be an inspiration to guide you in the discovery of the life God has planned for you and your spouse. John Burroughs offers, "No matter how often a man fails, he is not a failure until he starts blaming someone else." A marriage requires two people working together who will, in the course of pursuing happiness, make mistakes—mistakes not viewed as failures but as fuel for the future. When we learn from our mistakes, we fuel the possibilities our future holds.

How do we conform our will to the will of our Father in heaven? Through character and competence. Steven Covey states, "Character is who we are, competence is what we can do, both are necessary." In order to conform our will, we need two essential ingredients—the first being character. We must have the character to live by the decisions we have made and stand for the issues in which we believe.

Greg and Sharon Dosmann are good friends of ours. From the moment Laura and I met them, I sensed we had much in common. Over time the four of us have spent a lot of time together in social activities and community and Christian service. Greg had a problem that could be annoying at times, however. Punctuality.

Greg lives life to the fullest and tries to get the most out of every moment. As a result, he often scheduled too many appointments, started too many projects, or made too many phone calls for the amount of time allotted. He was consistently late for commitments.

If we were going out to dinner at 6:00 P.M., we started telling Greg that we were leaving at 5:45, so he would be on time. If a meeting was slated for 7:00, we'd tell Greg 6:30 so he'd arrive early. Sharon was frustrated by this behavior as much as everyone else.

Then one day Greg miraculously changed! I'm not sure what transpired in his life. Maybe he missed a big appointment, maybe he forgot a birthday, or maybe he just realized change was eminent. But one day, he climbed into his car, drove to the Franklin Covey store, purchased the deluxe "plan the rest of your life" organizer, and actually used it. Now, Greg Dosmann is one of the most organized individuals I know. He never misses meetings or appointments, and is rarely late for anything. Why? He conformed his will.

Our will is at our disposal to govern as we please. We know what to do, we know all the right answers. It is up to our will to make the decision to rise up and take action. Like Greg, we have a choice to never be the same again and literally change the pattern of our lives forever.

The same principle is true in our marriages. We know we should date our wives, we know we shouldn't nag our husbands, we know all the "right" things that need to be done. Now the question is, will we conform our will to the pattern of this world which is constantly telling us to take the easy way out, or are we prepared to make the right choice—the tough choice—and accomplish what we know needs to be done?

The process of conforming our will involves selecting the right choices, based solely on the fact that they are the correct choices, and then act. Between thinking and acting lies the critical step of conforming our will. It takes courage. Courage is not the absence of fear, courage is fear turned inside out. It is impossible to be courageous if at first you weren't afraid.

Perform Acts of Service

"Offer your bodies as living sacrifices…which is your spiritual worship." There is nothing more you can do to bring about abundant life than to offer your body. To truly serve our spouse exemplifies Christ's greatest challenge: "Greater love has no one than this, that he lay down his life for his friends" (John 15:13 NIV).

Natasha, a twelve-year-old girl who lived in Russia during the rise of communism, was a Christian who loved Jesus with all of her heart. Then came the day she would choose to lay down her life. The church was perceived to be the enemy of the State, and anyone who attended a church service was considered the enemy and sentenced to die. History will mark several atrocities performed upon unsuspecting souls during this time. Legend has it that frequently squads of soldiers would burst into churches on Sunday mornings and open fire as people sat in worship.

On this particular Sunday, however, the soldiers who burst into Natasha's small country church didn't open fire. Instead, they decided to play a game with the parishioners. The captain made his way to the front and pushed the pastor out of the pulpit. He then motioned to one of his men to remove the picture of Jesus from the wall and carry it to the back of the church.

He addressed the congregation saying: "Today you have a choice. You may get up from your seats, renounce your faith, spit on the picture of Jesus and go free, or sit here and die." He looked at his pocket watch and coldly said, "Two minutes."

Immediately people rose and walked to the back, renounced their faith and spit upon the picture of Jesus, then walked out the door to freedom. Mothers with small children began to weep, wondering; "Do I renounce my faith and save my child or remain seated and be responsible for both of our deaths?"

After a few moments, Natasha rose, walked to the back of the church, and picked up the picture of Jesus. Turning back to the pulpit, she slowly walked forward and as she did, she took the hem of her dress and wiped the spit off the picture. Standing face to face with the captain, Natasha stared into his eyes filled with hate, anger, and evil. As he looked at the young girl, the captain saw in her eyes peace, joy, and love.

"Sir," Natasha began, "you can take away my life, but you can never take away my Jesus!" With those strong yet loving words, the captain and his men were moved. They proceeded to put away their guns and walked away, never to be seen in that part of the country again.

This simple story illustrates the power that lies in the action of laying down one's life. When we give up—when we do not have to win—we allow the Holy Spirit to work. When the strain of always saving face is eliminated and we authentically strive to serve our spouse, we grow deeper in our relationship and our marriages change. This isn't change by any human means lest any single individual may boast, but change that can only come from divine intervention as God moves in our midst.

When was the last time you laid down your life for your spouse? When was the last time you ignored your carefully planned agenda to serve your family? Didn't seek a compromise so that you'd both get your way, but just served? Service is the means by which we lay down our lives for our spouse. We offer our bodies as we perform acts of service in honor of the example Christ gave us when He gave His life for us.

Why not . . .

+ Share some ways you've seen your thinking transformed over the years.

+ Choose one habit that needs changing. Share that habit with your spouse and ask him or her to hold you accountable to the change.

+ Look for secret opportunities to perform acts of service for your spouse that will never be detected. Let this be a form of worship unto the Lord.

Seven

You Gotta
Lose

As a speaker, I have the opportunity to communicate in many different arenas. One of my favorites is the business community. I am privileged as a guy with a youth ministry background to guide men and women through principles that will improve their business and productivity. Part of the fun is that I am still a youth minister at heart, so my presentations are generally filled with enthusiastic activities interspersed with various hands-on learning opportunities.

One of my favorite interactive activities involves bringing two women to the front of the gathering and introducing them to the challenge of arm wrestling. Facing their opponent, the women sit, arms clenched, ready for battle. Friendship among the participants often facilitates fierce competition without the threat of daggers. The clock is set for one minute and the objective is to see how many times they can defeat the other person. Working the ladies into a WWF big-time wrestling frenzy, I split the crowd into two cheering sections to support the participants.

As the crowd cheers, perspiration will begin to form as these ladies give their all to claim the victory. If I'm lucky, the women will work and strain and end up deadlocked without a winner for a full minute. Occasionally, one of the warriors will overpower their opponent and win three or four battles in the course of the minute. Regardless of the outcome, the trap has been set.

At the conclusion of the battle, I ask the audience which participant won. If one lady was stronger, then the answer is obvious. If they were deadlocked, the answer is "Nobody won." The application: In business, is it ever good for there to be no winner? Obviously in our twenty-first century western mindset, the answer is no.

After this match, I request one of the ladies to remain on stage and arm wrestle with me (carefully choosing my adversary). To aid my cause, I tell her that no matter how pumped she thinks she might be, she won't beat me. I will bust a blood vessel in order to beat her...my male ego...blah, blah, blah. My guest is then asked, "Do you believe I can beat you?" "Yes," comes the response. Then I look her square in the eye and say, "Trust me." I grab her hand with a good deal of force then I relax, to show her that I am worthy of her trust.

As we begin to do battle, I pull her hand down on top of mine and say, "You win," then I quickly move our hands to the other side of the table and say, "I win." Back and forth, back and forth. Within 20 seconds, we have both won so many times we lose count, and forget that we've also lost equally as many rounds. The joy of working together far outweighs the cost of "losing." Not only is this a great lesson for the business community; it is a tremendous reality in marriage. In the best marriages we "lay down our life," i.e., lose for the good of the union.

"Who was the greatest loser of all time?" I sometimes ask, and receive a wide range of responses from "Hitler" and "Stalin" to "my ex-husband."

Let's consider the words of Paul in Philippians 2:5-7: "Your attitude should be the same as that of Christ Jesus: Who, being in very nature God, did not consider equality with God something to be grasped, but made himself nothing, taking the very nature of a servant, being made in human likeness" (NIV).

Of particular note is the phrase "Jesus…made himself nothing." Remember that Jesus is God in heaven. He had legions of angels at his beck and call, and chose to make himself nothing. Not smaller, not a little, not something less than God, but *nothing*. Jesus lost more than any one of us could ever imagine, thereby making Him the greatest loser of all time.

Conversely, Jesus is also the greatest winner of all time. Continuing in verses 9 to 11: "Therefore God exalted him to the highest place and gave him the name that is above every name, that at the name of Jesus every knee should bow, in heaven and on earth and under the earth, and every tongue confess that Jesus Christ is Lord, to the glory of God the Father."

Encouragement in Christ

By coming to earth, Jesus demonstrated for us the meaning of the word "selfless." Out of that selflessness, He was exalted and given the name above every name. You, too, can be selfless by putting into action Paul's words from Philippians 2:1: "If you have any encouragement from being united with Christ…"

Encouragement is one of the most valuable words in the English language. The word literally means "to give courage." Whether we realize it or not, when we offer encouragement, particularly to our spouse, we actually fill their tanks with the courage it may take to face a difficult task or the day at hand.

I relish being an encourager. In recent years, I've had the pleasure of coaching our men's church league basketball team. While I am not a basketball genius, nor particularly gifted in the art of placing the ball through the cylinder, I enjoy participating in any game that comes along.

My coaching style is relatively simple: Make sure everyone has an opportunity to play, and praise individuals when they play well or do something right. Usually by the end of the game I'm hoarse from shouting encouragements at the team from the bench.

All of us enjoy being encouraged, particularly by someone we respect. Nothing gets my juices flowing like a high five from a teammate after making a three-point shot or a great pass. Encouragement crosses socioeconomic and ethnic boundaries and has the potential to create bonds that last a lifetime. That's why it is so vital to a healthy marriage. When we "lose" ourselves, and give courage to our spouse, we lift ourselves as we lift them.

Sometimes merely finishing is winning!

Directing Colorado Challenge has caused more great life lessons to slap me in the face than any other activity in my life. Every year my good friend Doug Laman poses to the entire camp what he calls "The Ultimate Challenge." The objective is simple: Run without stopping two miles down the mountain road, then turn around and run back up, for a total of four miles. The point is not who can do it the fastest, but who can complete the trip without stopping. Over the years, the popularity of encouraging your peers to accept the challenge has soared. The trip down is a breeze; even the weakest of runners (insert "Jay") can scrounge up the energy to run the two-mile stretch down the mountain with relative ease. The pace is steady and quick. Doug does a great job of organizing water and encouragement stations to facilitate the runners' progress. Dotted along the road, the cheering section greets us by throwing water in our faces, generally soaking us to the skin. In the warm mountain air, the water bath is a cool and refreshing experience. There is little time for dialogue as we swiftly descend the road.

Our attitudes change in a heartbeat, however, as we touch the fence at the bottom of the mountain and begin the 1000-foot dirt road ascent back to camp while maneuvering multiple switchbacks. For Midwestern flatlanders the physical challenge can be overwhelming.

Within 100 yards of turning around, many participants begin to walk. In the first quarter mile the elevation changes dramatically and each runner compensates by slowing their pace to a crawl. Keep in mind, the goal is not who finishes first, but to finish without stopping. Slowly advancing past youthful runners, I can practically read their minds. "He's old, he's fat, and he's passing me…let me die right here!"

The people manning the water stations have now transformed from playful water throwers to hard working co-laborers assisting our ascent. Most of the kids I passed as they walked have caught their second wind, and I am once again near the back of the pack. My mind focuses on reaching the next watering station, longing for contact with the source of my energy. A hundred yards from the next oasis, I encounter a smiling face and two cups of water—one for my head and one for my mouth. "Mom Ellis," as she's known to the youth, points up the hill and says, "Just a little farther and you'll pass the first station." My quadriceps locate some reserve energy and I plug away. Some of the people at the water stations would run with us for a while, then turn around and join the next person charging up the hill. All in all they probably ran the same distance, yet did not receive the credit for completing the challenge.

Every time I thought another step was impossible, I would come within earshot of another encourager prodding me to journey a little bit farther. Arriving at the summit, I embraced each encourager with a sweaty but heartfelt hug. They had no idea that their words made the difference between finishing and not completing the climb.

Everyday we have an opportunity to encourage our spouse with words and actions. How often do we take the time to reflect on the "race" that they are running? Our encouragement may be the difference in helping them reach the summit of their particular mountain.

Every individual needs encouragement in a unique way. Ask your spouse what you do or say that gives them the encouragement they need to continue. Make a mental note to say or do those things as often as you can.

Consolation of Love

Some people know how to console and do it naturally and effortlessly. For others of us, however, the term "sympathy" rarely enters our vocabulary. Particularly for the type "A" driven personality, it seems as though we rarely exhibit the same comfort of love we have received in Christ. For a select few, consolation is instinctive.

The 1984 Summer Olympics were held in Los Angeles, California. Derek Redmond was one of Great Britain's brightest hopes for an Olympic medal. He was a superb athlete with a sculpted body, which ran like the wind. But tragedy struck the life of Derek Redmond that summer. Making his way through the qualifying heats, he was in the lead of a particular race. Heading around the final turn and kicking his body into high gear for the stretch run, Derek suddenly collapsed, grasping his hamstring. As he lay in agonizing pain on the track, the other competitors raced by and crossed the finish line.

Immediately, race officials ran to Derek's side. Pushing them aside he struggled to his feet. Barely able to walk, Derek made his way toward the finish line. Step, step, stumble, fall. Step, step, stumble, fall. Others ran to his side and again, he pushed them away. Step, step, stumble, fall. Again the help came, and Derek refused, determined to finish this race.

Slowly, a figure began to climb over the edge of the stadium seats. At first, no one noticed as all eyes were focused on the drama on the track. Then a large man in a white T-shirt entered the view of the cameras. As the lens focused in on the looming figure, the words "DEREK'S DAD" practically leaped off the front of the man's shirt. Firm and sure, the father reached toward his son. Derek looked up and took hold of the man who loved him more than anyone else in the world. Together, they walked across the finish line.

We all stumble, we all fall. We all have points in our lives where we cannot walk without the assistance of another human being. When we "lose" ourselves and reach out in a compassionate love, we learn the power of finishing the race together.

What is our response when we watch our spouse fall? Do we criticize? Do we convict? Or do we console? "But what they did hurt me!" True, it is easy for one spouse to hurt another, but I will never forget a lesson from my father. "Son, understand this," he said, "hurting people hurt people." Frequently, the hurt we feel is born out of the pain experienced by the person performing the hurtful deed.

Take a moment to reflect on this passage of Scripture. "Bear with each other and forgive whatever grievances you may have against one another. Forgive as the Lord forgave you" (Colossians 3:13 NIV). What better place to practice the art of consoling (forgiveness) than with our spouse. Why do we forgive? Because the Lord has forgiven us.

Once, after a particularly hurtful time in our marriage, I asked Laura why she was able to forgive me so easily. She quickly responded, "Trust me, it's not of my own doing. It's only because I know how much God has forgiven me!" Her consolation and forgiveness fostered healing in our marriage.

Fellowship of the Spirit

Have you ever been in a situation where you unquestionably knew that the Spirit of the Lord was present and you didn't want to leave a place. For us, Quaker Ridge Camp in Woodland Park, Colorado, where we hold our annual Colorado Challenge Camp for teens, is an example of such a place.

Every summer kids from across the country travel to Quaker Ridge for what we affectionately call "a week-long Mountain Dew Commercial." Whitewater rafting, mountain biking, rock climbing, and rappelling are only a portion of the challenges teens enjoy. The evening hours host a session where a musician and speaker lead us in praise, worship, and teaching.

I don't know if it's the altitude or the atmosphere or the water, but something about Colorado Camp helps one encounter the Holy Spirit in a real and personal way. Teens and counselors alike experience an extraordinary mountaintop experience. I truly believe the key ingredient is the fellowship.

Most of the staff that frequent Colorado Challenge have either been bringing kids for five or more years, or attended themselves as high school students. It is unbelievable how people from diverse backgrounds instantaneously bond, especially after traveling for 24 straight hours in a van or bus. The function of camp is that kids who never knew each other before this week walk away with life-long friendships. Many tears and even more hugs are exchanged before the vans head home on Saturday morning.

This level of fellowship is what each of us should desire to experience in our lives. It is the treasure for which our souls search. Once found, we never want to let it go. All too often our attachment is to the event or place rather than the spirit of Christ who bonds us in fellowship.

In marriage, experiencing this level of fellowship is critical. When we "lose" ourselves, our ambitions, our preferences, and our agendas and seek sincere fellowship, we experience a place we never want to leave. Finding this fellowship is possible only when we rely on the spirit of Jesus Christ and enter into His presence in corporate worship.

"But my spouse won't go with me to church!" is often a resounding cry. Perhaps one of the biggest lies of Satan is that "worship can take place only on Sunday morning." How sad. Worship is perpetual. We can worship the one true living God anywhere, anyplace, and anytime.

For example, the next time you and your spouse are traveling by car and you see a beautiful sight through the window or hear an inspiring song, comment on the beauty or the depth of the words of the song, and in your spirit invite the Holy Spirit to join you. In that moment, you and your spouse will be worshiping together and your spouse may not even know it. This will be an opportunity for you to bring him or her into the presence of the Lord—the essence of all worship. Ask the Lord to give you the words as He directs through verbal and non-verbal communication.

Affection

While in Romania, I learned a powerful lesson. One of the most striking memories for me was the way the people touched each other, a genuine definite love and affection flowing between them.

The men all greeted each other with the classic European kiss on each cheek, a custom I've observed many times on the silver screen or the tube, but never personally. Initially, I was taken back. As a heterosexual man I couldn't understand affection between two men without sexual overtones. The more I experienced this tradition, however, the more I grew to appreciate the depth of feeling reflected by this act. For the European, it is the ultimate expression of brotherly love.

The Romanian women take this affection a step further, by holding hands, locking arms, and walking closely together. Little girls practicing this custom were not uncommon to me. Then I caught a glimpse of a couple of elderly women and thought, "That looks odd." But when I saw two teenagers locking arms, I questioned my interpreter, "What is going on here?" "Oh," he commented, "they're best friends."

Throughout the city, I observed women walking arm in arm in the kind of embrace you'd expect with newlyweds here in the States. The little girls were cute, and my mind justified that the elderly relied on each other for support as they walked, but when the teens embraced, my western mindset immediately assumed they were lesbians. Upon frequently observing this behavior, I made the assumption that there was a large lesbian population in Romania. My interpreter just laughed that you-stupid-American kind of laugh to which I'd become accustomed soon after arriving in the country.

The Romanian women denote their best friend by walking in public arm in arm. If my wife and her friends sauntered down Superior Street locked arm in arm, they would be the talk of the town. But in Romania it is a outward display of sincere and heartfelt affection.

Without a doubt, our western heritage, with all of its benefits, has really shortchanged us in the department of affection. I think we could all learn a lesson from the Romanians, and put affectionate actions back into our daily lifestyles. When we "lose" ourselves and begin to show our spouse the heartfelt love they deserve, we may lose a bit of our rugged American individuality, but in the end we will win the heart of the one we love.

Ask your spouse this question: What do I do that makes you feel loved? Their answer will give you insight into the level of affection they need. (If you're real gutsy, ask them what you do that makes them feel unloved? This will shed a whole new light on your relationship.)

Compassion

Joneen Wight, a woman as unique as her name might imply, is my best friend and one of the most compassionate people you will ever meet. A true servant of others, she is constantly championing the cause of the less fortunate. Blessed with the gift of hospitality, she can bake a pie with the best of them. She loves all creatures great and small, particularly her "grand-dog."

Joneen and her husband Russ have one daughter, Amy Jo, who is married to a wonderful young man named Phil. Before Phil and Amy Jo had kids, they bought a dog, Carly, who Joneen immediately dubbed her "grand-dog." You'd think this dog had come from her own loins the way she cares and caters to it. While Joneen would admit she gets somewhat carried away, the reality of the matter is that she is an expert at demonstrating compassion. Whether it's Carly, a hurting teenager in town, or an elderly woman who just needs a friend, Joneen has the unique ability to put herself in the shoes (or paws) of another being, and not only walk a mile, but feel every stone and blister along the way.

This is the function of compassion. Compassion is not feeling sorry for someone. Compassion is feeling what another feels and then acting in a way that helps the person handle their particular situation.

When we demonstrate compassion, we "lose" ourself in the graciousness of the act and find that, in the end, we win by creating an atmosphere where true love is shown. Our marriages are built on mutual struggle and accomplishment, not on the back of one partner or at the expense of the other.

Encourage each other in Christ.

Console each other in love.

Fellowship with each other in the Spirit.

Demonstrate affection and compassion.

Become selfless in your marriage and experience the joy of winning that "losing" brings.

Why not . . .

- ✦ Discuss the importance of winning in your life.
- ✦ Define the cost of losing for you.
- ✦ Choose an attribute from the list above and commit together to "losing" yourselves in that attribute.

Eight

You Gotta
Linger

YFC

*A*ll through my high school and college days, I swore I would never be employed by the organization to which my father had devoted his life. Youth for Christ is a wonderful evangelistic organization which has touched the lives of millions of kids and their families. Though growing up in the organization, I felt any involvement on my part would be eternally connected with my dad's reputation.

Willie and Virginia Foote are lifers in YFC just like my mom and dad. Willie was the director in Atlanta and Virginia handled many different tasks in the office. At our wedding, Willie asked Laura and me if we had considered working in YFC. He invited us to attend a ministry event in Gatlinburg, Tennessee, to check out what was going on in the Southern Region of YFC. We accepted his offer, and following our time in Gatlinburg, began to consider the pros and cons of employment in the ministry.

All this time, the words "I'll never work for YFC" echoed through my mind and I prepared to eat some serious crow! The bottom line for Laura and me was the fact that we were committed to minister together. Furthermore, the interim jobs we had in the mall were going nowhere fast.

Gwinnett County

Laura and I were assigned the task of building an evangelistic youth ministry from scratch in the fastest growing county in the U.S.A. Simultaneously thrilling and frightening, the Lord seemed to fling open one door and slam another shut almost daily. Within eighteen months, we had scratched and clawed our way into a pretty good position in the area. Gwinnett County Campus Life clubs were filling homes with upwards of 100 teenagers, and we were beginning to see the fruit of the 65 to 70 hours of work we dedicated to this fledgling ministry. We were also beginning to taste the bitter fruit of our overloaded schedules.

In the first two years of our marriage, I had gained over 25 pounds as McDonalds and Taco Bell meals on the run were standard fare. Laura was either working or sleeping all the time. We were totally out of balance. Finally, upon reviewing our lifestyle, it became clear that the "rat race" had to end.

The last year of ministry in Gwinnett County, we had outstanding volunteers, and many student leaders were excited about seeing their friends come to know Christ. Finally realizing a sense of balance, we joined the YMCA and reduced our work week to 55 to 60 hours. We still felt, however, that it was time to move on to a new ministry location.

Give Me An "A"

During the summer of 1987, we planned a vacation/job search in Michigan. Laura had fallen in love with the four-season splendor of my home state, and with an established track record within YFC, I didn't hesitate to return to walking in my dad's "shadow."

Through each interview, it became clear the Lord was directing us. The interview in Alma was unbelievable. Central Michigan Youth for Christ was a new start-up and with the diligent work of a dedicated steering committee, the groundwork for a charter had been completed.

I remember the expression on Mick Koutz's face as we entered the room for our initial meeting. He was smiling from ear to ear as though greeting a long lost friend. The mood was comfortable and the presence of the Lord genuinely permeated the room and alleviated any lingering anxiety. John Leppien, CMYFC's board chairman, noted the telephone number where we were vacationing and two days later, during a second interview, they offered us the position. Alma, Michigan became our hometown on October 1, 1987.

Acknowledging the enormous task in front of us, and with all the excitement of new ministry, Laura and I dove headfirst into the work in Alma. Before long we regressed into the destructive lifestyles we had vacated in Atlanta. After tracking my hours our first three years in Central Michigan, I discovered my work week averaged 72 hours. Another problem complicating our life was that Laura and I neglected the four weeks of vacation negotiated in our employment agreement. We were firmly entrenched into the rat race again.

December of 1990 brought us a tremendous gift, Torrey, our son. Laura was back to work six weeks after delivery, and actually started attending school events and activities when Torrey was only two weeks old. Soon our son joined the "race."

Praise the Lord—and I mean PRAISE THE LORD—we finally began to recognize the long-term damage our lifestyle was inflicting. Laura and I rarely saw each other except when we fell exhausted into bed each night. My weight had ballooned to a downright fat 256 pounds, and Torrey was spending his waking hours in day care and with baby sitters.

The Mission

1993 was a pivotal year for us as we began to discern the course the Lord would have for our lives. We began the process of writing our Family Mission Statement and to discuss dreams and set goals we felt the Lord was specifically giving to us. I began to pursue speaking as a career.

I had been speaking publicly since high school, but in 1987 Laura and I took Ken Davis' Dynamic Communicators Workshop. It literally changed my life. The workshop gave me the tools necessary to speak confidently in groups of any size. From time to time I began to work speaking engagements into my schedule and dreamed of someday making a living doing the one thing I enjoyed most.

As we began to live in line with our family mission (a mission we felt was given by the Lord) we realized the ministry lifestyle of YFC was not going to mesh as our children began to grow. We knew a change was on the horizon.

In the mix of all this, a growing relationship was developing with Scott Davis and Jeff Klein with whom I had become great friends as a result of planning and directing the Colorado Challenge camp each summer. As we shared, prayed, and worked together throughout the year, we began to realize that most of what we were doing in ministry was in "our own" and not necessarily the Lord's strength. Don't get me wrong; the Lord was moving. Kids' lives were being changed. Yet ministers know when they are and are not relying on the Lord. Laura and I both were convinced that God didn't want us to *do* anything for Him; He simply wanted us to be *with* Him. Only then can the real work of the Spirit be accomplished. It was time to leave YFC.

Transition

I was taught to never leave a job undone. Our job offer in Alma came in July and we didn't move from Atlanta until October as we wanted to assure a smooth transfer of responsibility. The same was true in Alma. I didn't want to leave the ministry of CMYFC until we were able to facilitate a smooth transition that would allow the ministry to continue without interruption.

At our January board meeting, I tendered my resignation effective July 1, and began to seek the Lord for direction.

As we work with couples across the country, we see the devastating lifestyles that our demanding culture has created. If you desire to leave a legacy to your children and grandchildren, then you may realize it's time to get O.U.T.!

Observe

I call him "Pocket-change Jesus." He's the religious figure most Americans pull out of their pocket whenever they need a little help. He's like a "lucky coin," there only for our convenience. While many of us really don't think we treat Jesus this way, the truth is we have no idea of the majesty of our Lord. He is truly "Big Jesus" and we should stand in awe, wonder, and fear.

September 11, 2001. Most of us will never forget where we were that dreadful morning. It was Grace's fourth birthday, and we were celebrating with her "Aunt Joneen'" when the horror unfolded. In the days, weeks, and months that followed, America united under the phrase, "In God We Trust, United We Stand." Americans began looking for God to answer the big questions pre-empted by the tragedy. Churches were flooded with people seeking answers.

Economically, our leaders told us to keep doing what we would "normally" do as this was what the country needed. Unfortunately, in the months following September 11, Americans returned to "normal" spiritually as they found little comfort in our "pocket-change Jesus." The Jesus they saw didn't make sense; He was simply too small to meet their needs, answer their questions, and heal the hurt.

We must linger with the Lord. The first step in getting out of the rat race and really enjoying marriage is to observe the greatness of our God. We must understand that Jesus is the great Creator God Almighty. He spoke and the universe spun into place. "Let there be" and there was—the universe and everything in it as a testimony to the Creator. Stop for a moment and observe the greatness of our God. He is mighty, magnificent, and majestic. Observing His greatness will strike a holy fear which the psalmist says is the "beginning of wisdom" (111:10 NIV).

I believe the best psychotherapy is experiencing the wonder of nature. We change when we visit oceans, mountains, or forests. We change primarily because of the majesty; we stand in awe of the creation, and subsequently the Creator. Unfortunately, the urbanization of America has done a similar but drastically different thing to our psyche. We stand in the middle of a beautiful city with skyscrapers and detailed architecture and marvel at both the creation and the creator. The result is that we have slowly but surely lost our need for God. We can see all, do all, and be all that we really need. We're self-sufficient, or so we think. We muddle along through this world thinking we do not need God and settle for less than His best.

When we observe gently falling snow as it blankets the ground, we are reminded of how God's grace has covered us with the purity of His love. When we gaze at a mountain with its entire splendor, we must recognize it is just a glimpse of the majesty of the Almighty. When we observe the pounding waves on the seashore we must realize the power of the ocean compared to the weakness of man, and we know that the God who crafted the ocean waves is larger than life itself, so much bigger than we ever imagined. Then and only then do we begin to linger, to stop momentarily and fathom as Solomon did that all we chase after is meaningless. " 'Meaningless! Meaningless!' says the Teacher. 'Utterly meaningless! Everything is meaningless.' What does man gain from all his labor at which he toils under the sun?" (Ecclesiastes 1:2-3 NIV).

We chase after a vapor and fail to realize the value of the greatest earthly gift we have—each other. Linger with your spouse today, enjoy just being together. Take some time with no agenda, no itinerary, and spend time together. While at first it may be difficult to mesh your schedules, the reward will be a miraculous power unfolding before your eyes as you observe the wonder and majesty of the Lord and begin to identify true priorities for your life together.

Understand Your Sin

Most of us spend our time either running from a past we cannot change or running toward a future that is uncertain, instead of running with God, the giver of life. Not until we admit we are totally powerless over sin will we truly begin to allow God's Spirit to work in us and demonstrate the meaning of a full life. The first step is to understand our sin nature.

The Turtle and the Scorpion

In the forest lived a turtle and a scorpion. Every day around noon the scorpion would wander down to the stream for a drink. Every day the scorpion would observe a turtle swim by and stop on a rock in the middle of the stream to sun himself. The scorpion often wondered what it would be like to sit on the warm rock with the cool stream rushing by.

One day the scorpion shouted to the turtle, "Come here, sir." Cautiously the turtle swam to the edge of the stream, but not so close as to get stung. "I was wondering," asked the scorpion, "if one day you would be so kind as to take me over to that rock so that I might enjoy the mid-day sun and cool stream." "How absurd," replied the turtle. "Why, if I get too close to you, you will sting me and I would die." "Well," the scorpion said, "what if we met downstream, down where the rocks jut out into the stream. I'll come out on the rocks and you can swim by. I'll hop on your back, and then you can drop me at the big rock in the middle. There is no way I'd sting you as I would perish too." The turtle examined the plan from all angles, couldn't see a problem, and agreed. "OK, tomorrow it will be."

Just before noon the next day, the scorpion skittered out on the rock peninsula to wait for his ferry ride on the back of the turtle. A few moments later, the turtle swam up to the edge of the peninsula and the scorpion jumped on. About halfway to the big rock, the scorpion inched his way to the front of the turtle's shell and, with a quick spike of its tail, stung the turtle on the back of his neck, sending deadly venom into the bloodstream of the turtle.

Almost immediately the turtle felt the paralyzing effects of the venom and his ability to swim was quickly fading. Just before both the turtle and scorpion were about to submerge, ending their lives, the turtle looked back at the scorpion and said; "Why did you sting me? Now we will both perish." To which the scorpion replied, "It's just my nature to sting."

A simple story with a profound message: For us, sin is just our nature. As a result we must recognize the need to battle sin every day, particularly in our marriage. The Bible clearly states that we "all have sinned and fall short of the glory of God" (Romans 3:23 NIV). Virtually every day our sin nature will cause us to act selfishly or in a hurtful manner. Understanding our sin allows us to admit that we are powerless over it and as we daily surrender that weakness, we allow the grace of God to flow through us, making us more like Christ

Marriage is the perfect proving ground for living a life of undenied weakness and reliance on the Lord as the source of our strength.

Throw Out the Junk

It amazes me how much junk one family can accumulate over the years. Laura and I have survived two major household moves in our marriage. I guess that's few by today's standards, but each time we moved, I was overwhelmed by the junk that we had accumulated. Even after the moving sale we found ourselves holding up a piece of plastic something and asking the question, "What in the world is this?" My textbook retort, "Throw it out!"

Wouldn't it be nice if it were that easy to throw out the junk, the garbage, and the unnecessary baggage in our marriages? Change is never that easy, however. Change occurs only when a couple becomes frustrated with the status quo. If one spouse is "satisfied" with the way things are, then change rarely happens. In those moments when dissatisfaction with the accumulation of junk occurs, take action immediately.

Why not sit down with your spouse and make a list of those things that have crept into your marriage. Take a "junk inventory" and see what can be thrown out. The "junk" could include habits or actions that you have fallen into as a couple that have been detrimental to your relationship. For example, some couples develop a routine of going to bed at different times. For some that may not be a bad thing; however, for us that would create havoc. If I went to bed every night at eight o'clock and read until I feel asleep, and if this became the norm in our marriage, we would never spend any time alone, intimate or not. Many years ago we decided that we wouldn't go to bed without the other person, unless due to illness.

The word "linger" brings to mind the picture of a wide front porch with huge rocking chairs, a warm breeze, and two people enjoying each other's company. That is what God designed us to do in our marriages. Take time to linger with your spouse. Take time to enjoy each other. Get out and sit on the front porch. Feel the breeze blow in your face and linger together!

Why not...

+ Take some time away in nature and reconnect with the Creator.
+ Confess unrepented sin in your life right now.
+ Make a list of the "junk" in your marriage that you are responsible for and then throw it out.

Nine

You Gotta
Lead

The Pin

*I*t was early spring in Michigan. The snow that had been plowed during the winter rested in large piles on the edges of the parking lot at Meridian Mall in East Lansing. During the day, the warm springtime sun magically melted the towering snow-drifts, spreading a thin layer of water across the asphalt.

At night, the freezing temperatures formed a thin layer of ice on the blacktop. "Black ice" is a major concern for motorists in the upper Midwest at this time of year, as it is not easily detected by the naked eye. You simply can't see it. It can send your car into a tailspin faster than you can say Jack Frost, and can send a pedestrian to their fanny just as quick.

My mother was on her way to the mall to return some gifts. Not noticing the black ice, the next thing she knew, she was on the ground holding her leg. As she came to her senses, she realized the severity of the injury to her leg.

Dad and I were in Cadillac, Michigan, at a meeting with other YFC directors when the phone rang. The Cadillac director called Dad to the phone, then told me, "Jay, I think your mom's hurt; she's calling from the hospital." When Dad returned he shared the news.

Mom had slipped on the ice, and a fraction of a second later, her foot hit a clean patch of pavement. The force and torque of her movements were so violent, that she broke her leg in ten places between her knee and her ankle. By the time she called us, she had already gone through surgery and had been placed in a Minelli-Spinelli device.

The Minelli-Spinelli was an interesting contraption consisting of two metal plates that encircled Mom's leg, one just below the knee and the other just above the ankle. Attached to the plates were ten surgical pins that traveled through the leg and were held in place by setscrews. The pins literally pierced her leg like the bolts on the side of Frankenstein's neck.

The doctors had told her that as little as 10 to 5 years earlier, they would have had to amputate her leg due to the severity of the break. Further, she was informed, she would probably always walk with a limp and might require the use of a cane or walker for the rest of her life.

Every Monday, Dad drove Mom to the doctor's office for an X-ray to see if the bone fragments were aligning. If a bone was out of place, the doctor would loosen a couple of setscrews and adjust the position of the bone fragment inside the leg. The doctors told them that she would be in this device for six weeks, and then they'd talk about the next step.

Daily, Dad had the arduous task of cleaning the 14 pin sites. The doctor made it clear that if bacteria entered the wound via the pin sites, the resulting bone infection could lead to an amputation. As the "A" word was a concern from the start, extra care was given to the cleaning process. Morning and evening, in his pursuit of health for his wife, Dad would sit on his knees with Mom's leg in front of him and two bright lights shining over his shoulders.

Cleaning the pin sites was a 30-minute process as three separate cleaning solutions were used on each site. The first would dissolve the residue scab which had formed around the pin. The second was an antiseptic to clean the site, and the third, a gummy substance to seal the wound.

The doctor explained to us that the bones of the lower leg are known as "dumb bones." Because they have less muscle or tissue surrounding them, they do not get as much blood flow as other bones and, as a result, they do not heal as fast. Because of this, Mom's leg would be required to remain in the Minelli-Spinelli indefinitely.

Finally, nine months after the accident, the Minelli-Spinelli was removed. The miracle of it all is that Mom now walks totally unassisted and without any evidence of a limp. On cool summer evenings, you can find my mom and dad, hand in hand, enjoying the simple pleasure of a walk around their subdivision.

As I look back on this situation, I see a trait in Dad that was perfected in our Lord Christ Jesus—leadership. Sure, from time to time, his attitude was less than spectacular. And from time to time he wanted to quit but, in his pursuit of excellence and dedication to perseverance, he focused not on the present difficulties (a broken leg) but on the future glory (a totally healed limb).

This story is a great example of leadership. Each of us should strive to be leaders in our homes. You can become a leader by following Christ's example given in Philippians 2:5-8.

> *Your attitude should be the same as that of Christ Jesus:*
> *Who, being in very nature God, did not consider equality*
> *with God something to be grasped, but made himself noth-*
> *ing, taking the very nature of a servant, being made in*
> *human likeness. And being found in appearance as a man,*
> *he humbled himself and became obedient to death—even*
> *death on a cross!* (NIV)

Be Emptied

Every relationship we have—whether with a spouse, our children, a friend or a business associate—will journey through four stages. For the sake of our discussion, we will look at these stages at they pertain to achieving union in our marital relationship.

The first stage is the *honeymoon* stage. We are in love; neither person can do anything wrong and forgiveness comes easy. Your heart skips a beat every time your loved one enters the room. As the relationship grows, the second stage *chaos* develops. The children have arrived. Your marriage is maturing, becoming settled. Routines begin to solidify. Your heart may not always skip a beat when your love walks into the room. In order to achieve unity, we have to enter the third stage, "to be emptied." We have to come to a point in our lives when we say "It isn't all about me." We have to put aside our individual agendas, desires, and needs to focus on our partner. Then, and only then, will we achieve unity, the fourth stage. In this stage we must strive to work together rather than against each other.

For most of us, the root of the problem is *pride*. Slice it up any way you wish but it usually boils down to a pride issue. We see leadership as the world does, and no matter how often we study this passage about Christ, we still can't get it right. Leadership is not about who is strongest or smartest or loudest; It's about who is willing to be like Christ.

Jesus Christ was unquestionably God. He had everything. "Who being in very nature God…" Can anyone honestly question His position?

Jesus then made Himself nothing. Not smaller, not littler, not tiny. Nothing, nil, nix, nada. At what point in my life have I done that? Okay. Never.

The New American Standard Version says, "Emptied Himself." Gave up every right associated with His supreme position as the Son of God. If we are going to lead, we must give up our rights, our privileges, and our entitlements in order to become more like Christ. What is interesting about this scenario is that the more we empty ourselves, the more room there is within us for Him.

As my dad served my mom during her rehabilitation, this principle became evident in his life like never before. It seemed as though the more he served Mom and her needs, the more he emptied himself and the more he became like Christ.

As you seek to be a leader in your family, start by being emptied.

Be Humbled

If we don't humble ourselves, life has a way of doing it for us. So we might as well do the humbling ourselves, or else...

In the summer of 1985 I found myself attending YFC's ministry training institute held every summer at Rockford College in Illinois. Laura and I had been approached at our wedding by the Atlanta YFC director about pioneering a new ministry in the fastest growing county in the U.S. The prospect of working with my bride and being 1,000 miles from my father's shadow was all the push I needed to give it a try.

I am a game guy. You need a game; I'll come up with one for us to play. I have never had a problem with remembering fun games to play and/or designing a new one on the spot. Thus I was bored and feeling a little self-assured when we finally reached the section of the training that dealt with group games.

Now, before you get all high and mighty wondering why in the world we would need training in group games, I challenge you to organize 80 to 100 kids into a fun and engaging activity without people getting a) hurt or b) bored. It is difficult and challenging work. But, not for Jay "Game Guy" Laffoon.

We were playing a game called "Out of the Pits." We divided the kids into groups of eight or ten and when the leader said, "Go," one student laid down flat on his back on the floor. As quickly as the group could, they lifted that student to head height, and then lowered him gently to the floor. This process was repeated until all members of the team had been lifted "Out of the Pits."

In the middle of playing this game (which I had played 100 times if I'd played it once), I was feeling cocky and arrogant as we bent down to lift a particularly large man off the floor. Then...rip! Everyone in the room heard it. It wasn't a gentle tearing of the garment. It was a stem-to-stern rip of my shorts. The sound stopped everyone in the room—all 60 of them—in their tracks. Because everyone there was training to be in youth ministry, we were all a little demented to begin with, but the trainer had to find out who had ripped his pants so he could take advantage of the guilty party.

As I was being ushered to the front of the room for the full examination, terror struck my heart in anticipation of the coming dilemma. You see, I had been practicing (along with all the other men at the training) a technique called "commando" in which you choose (for whatever reason I still do not understand) not to wear underwear. I stood in front of this class of youth ministers baring it all.

Life will humble us all so we might as well choose, as Christ did, to humble ourselves. In the long run it's a lot less embarrassing.

Be Obedient

Bruce Wilkinson tells the story of a woman who was planning to be a missionary to West Africa. As she prepared to go she visited garage sales to stock up on items she could take with her. She was to be a teacher in a school for boys. As she was perusing a sale, she distinctly heard the voice of God tell her to buy some soccer balls. She began to argue with the voice, but it continued to urge her to buy the balls. After a few minutes of arguing, she finally bought them, took them home, and packed them away with her stuff to go to West Africa.

When she eventually arrived at the school, she quietly entered a prayer meeting the boys were having. Her desire was to listen and observe the boys, giving her a true picture of her students. As she listened, she was touched by the way the boys prayed. One boy would shout out a topic and another boy would stand up and pray for that topic. As the missionary woman listened, she heard one boy shout out "soccer balls!" Another boy stood up praying for soccer balls, pleading their need for soccer balls for recess, practice and team sports.

The woman was astonished. She rose from her seat and went back to her room and retrieved the soccer balls that she had brought. As she entered the room where the boys were praying she tripped and the soccer balls fell out of her arms and down the center aisle. The boys were astonished! "How did God do that?!" one boy yelled out. How did God do that? Through the obedience of one woman.

How would the woman have felt if she had been sitting there in the prayer meeting and realized that she had left those soccer balls at a garage sale in America? What a blessing she received because of her obedience. Are we missing out on the blessings the Lord has for us in our marriage because of lack of obedience?

Why not...

+ Take a moment and discuss your definition of a leader.
+ Describe a time when you felt emptied...humbled...
+ What keeps you from total obedience to the Lord?

Ten

You Gotta
Be Led

I am the third of four children, two girls and two boys. I have a sister, Sandy, six years older than me. My brother Greg is four years older, and Tom is two years younger. There is some truth to the birth order theories! Sandy is definitely a firstborn. She is the boss. She is the meticulous one. She is the example the rest of us were supposed to follow. Greg is quiet, usually did his own thing, and really never bothered anybody. Tom is the typical baby of the family. He has had lots of practice batting those big blue eyes and getting whatever he wants. Everyone was always at his beck and call. I am the Third born child, lost in the crowd.

Sandy is feminine, I am a tomboy. Sandy talked on the phone at all hours to many boyfriends while I read books. Sandy never went out of the house without her makeup on and her hair done. Conversely, I didn't really care. She inherited our mother's ability to sew. And I could never sit still long enough to sew anything. While I love my sister dearly, growing up I knew we were different. We did not enjoy similar activities and I knew that I wasn't going to grow up to be like her.

When I was thirteen, Sandy married. I missed her incessantly, crying myself to sleep the night she left. I learned to appreciate having an older sister to protect me from our brothers. She took up for me when Mom couldn't understand why I was not "more like Sandy." Now I was on my own. I realized then that in order to survive, blazing my own trail was unavoidable and I became very independent.

Blazing your own trail is all well and good, until you want your trail to merge with another's.

Jay is a firstborn. He is the boss. He is the meticulous one. He is the leader. I had blazed my trail and developed some firstborn qualities over the years; therefore, I was not a very good follower. When my third-child-developing-first-child-tendencies trail converged with his first-child trail, some major adjustments followed.

Have you ever been driving down a dirt road after a good hard rain? You know those potholes that develop in the road from the downpour? As you are driving down the road, your chin is chattering, your arms are shaking, and your entire body is jiggling. Potholes can also develop in our marriages as we attempt to take two trails and make them one!

> "Honor Christ by submitting to each other. You wives must submit to your husbands' leadership in the same way you submit to the Lord" (Ephesians 5:21 LB).

I can submit to the Lord. He is the creator of the universe. Submit to my husband? He is merely a man! First pothole in my trail…

> "For a husband is in charge of his wife in the same way Christ is in charge of his body the church. (He gave his very life to take care of it and be its Savior)" (Ephesians 5:23 LB).

In charge of me…I am in charge of me! That pothole is becoming a crater!

> "So you wives must willingly obey your husbands in everything, just as the church obeys Christ." (Ephesians 5:24 TLB).

Willingly was a sinkhole…obey was the Grand Canyon!

For years I tried to explain away this passage...this only applies in a perfect world...yeah, like my husband is going to give up his life for me. When he does, I will obey...submit (obey is defined differently now...this is a new millennium!)

Ladies, it isn't easy. The stark reality is that Scripture commands it and we must practice it. These are the three realities that must be evident in our lives: Honor Christ by submitting to each other. Jesus put your husband in charge. We must willingly obey. It isn't easy, it is a daily challenge.

The first reality. It is worth repeating..."Honor Christ by submitting to each other's leadership. You wives must submit to your husbands' leadership in the same way you submit to the Lord." It starts out sounding good...we submit to each other...then Paul singles us out! "You wives..." I think that he knew this was going to be hard for us. Plain and simple, the buck stops with our husband. But this doesn't mean you live trampled underfoot like a doormat. Notice the first part of the verse says that we honor Christ by submitting to each other's leadership. There will be times the wife will know the best course of action. In our house, I am the barometer. I seem to know best when we need family time, or when Jay and I need some time alone. Jay listens to me and respects my leadership in these areas. As we all know, though, there will be those times that we come to an impasse over decisions that need to be made and we may have differing opinions. This is when I have to submit to my husband's leadership and respect the position in which the Lord has placed him. The buck stops with him.

One day, when our son Torrey was learning to tell his left hand from his right, I was trying to help him. I told TJ that I wished I could come up with a fun way for him to remember. He proceeded to tell me that his daddy had already done that: Put up your left hand and the thumb and fingers make an L for left. Put up your right hand and the thumb and fingers make a J because J is Daddy's name and he is always right! I laughed and laughed...then realized he was speaking the truth. It is very frustrating! 99.9 percent of the time Jay is right.

We each have been gifted by God with certain abilities and talents. We need to honor each other by recognizing those gifts and allowing each other to lead with their unique gifts.

The second reality. "For a husband is in charge of his wife in the same way Christ is in charge of his body the church." I can hear you...no one is in charge of me but me! Not true. If you call yourself a Christian, you gave those controls over to Jesus. He is in charge of your life. When you became a Christian you gave Him charge over you and you gave up running the show.

If you were to look up "charge" in the dictionary you would see the words "responsible," "safekeeping," "care," and "trust" are all a part of the definition. Jesus is telling me that Jay is responsible for me, he is to keep me safe, care for me. Jesus has put me into his hands, as did my parents on our wedding day.

Would you say as a parent that you are in charge of your children? Are they still individuals making up their own minds and making their own choices? The answer to both questions is yes. Now I am not implying that women are children, so don't stop reading.

My point is, take out that phrase "in charge" and replace it with "responsible." I can live with my husband being responsible for me. He takes care of me and sees that I have everything I need just as Jesus cares for the church. He makes sure that we are well-equipped to accomplish His will. Why do we always have to read this passage and think negative thoughts? Think positively!

"Husbands, love your wives, just as Christ loved the church and gave himself up for her" (Ephesians 5:25 NIV). Ladies, our husbands should be prepared to die for us! How cool is that! Submitting looks pretty easy compared to dying. Let's not be influenced by our world that says submission equals being treated like a doormat. Let us look at our Lord and Savior, who instructs us to allow our husbands to take care of us.

Jay frequently likes to joke with me that I'm a "kept woman." I reply with a hardy amen! When I was growing up, my image of a "kept woman" was someone who sat around and ate bon-bons, went to the club for lunch and bridge, spent the rest of the day shopping, and went home at night to lounge in a bubble bath! Hello, who wouldn't want to do that! Now, before you think that is what I do, let me set you straight. I don't like bon-bons! Seriously though, Jay says this because I allow him to do what the Lord has commanded him to do. Take care of me!

We must develop the ability to appreciate life from the half full point of view instead of half empty. Rejoice in the command the Lord has given us for our marriages. I fully believe that if we would allow our husbands to take care of us, submission would be less of an issue.

The third reality. *"You wives must willingly obey your husbands in everything just as the church obeys Christ." It isn't always easy to obey, let alone willingly! Why would I willingly obey a man who has such weird habits?*

I won't scare you with all the weirdness in the Laffoon family, but here is a taste. It is a new cure for the common cold! We had just arrived home from watching our niece play basketball. The kids were in bed and we were preparing a nighttime snack. I look over and Jay is bending over the sink, and with the running water, he is washing out his nose! Taking water in his hand, he shoves it up his nose, then he washes out his eyes and then his hands. (I would hope so!)

"Jay, honey, what are you doing?" He replies, "I am preventing the spread of germs. It is a proven fact that colds are spread through contact with other people, coming in contact with their germs." I laugh! He continues to inform me that he goes through this ritual whenever he has been around a lot of people. How paranoid! But no matter how weird I perceive him to be, the command is still the same...willingly obey.

> "For this reason a man will leave his father and mother
> and be united to his wife, and the two will become one
> flesh. This is a profound mystery—but I am talking about
> Christ and the church. However, each one of you also must
> love his wife as he loves himself, and the wife must respect
> her husband' (Ephesians 5:31-33 NIV).

It is our belief that Jesus gave us the gift of marriage as a microcosm of the body of Christ. Paul tells us the ultimate goal in marriage, i.e., leaving our parents and becoming one flesh. He follows this by saying, "Yes, this is a profound mystery, but actually I am not talking about marriage at all, but rather about the church and Jesus Christ." Finally he wraps his thoughts up by again reminding us again of our responsibilities in marriage: "Husbands love your wives and wives respect your husbands."

When all is said and done, all that matters is that you love and respect one another. Every discussion in your marriage, every pothole into which you may sink, every point of view that has two sides—it isn't about you and you alone. It is about the two of you together. We have missed the boat in Western evangelical culture because we have concentrated so much on individual relationships with Jesus Christ that we neglected the body life of the church. (But I won't get on that soap box, however; at least not in this volume.) Unfortunately, this attitude that the needs of the individual outweigh the needs of the family unit has permeated our marriages. It is about my *needs* and my *expectations* in our marriage.

For our relationships to be successful, the focus must center on "our," not me! It is our needs, our expectations, and our marriage.

Why not . . .

+ Read Ephesians, chapter 5, and pray, asking the Lord to give you His insight.

+ Discuss the roles that have emerged in your marriage.

+ What ones are good?

+ What ones need improving?

+ Discuss how your marriage aligns with the Ephesians chapter.

Eleven

You Gotta
Leave a
Legacy

The "C" word

The phone rang at 3 P.M. and my mom sounded concerned; "Jay, the doctor called and he wants to see me in his office. Jay, it can't be good news if he wants to see me in his office!" "Mom, I can drive down and go in with you if you want me to," I told her. "Naaaw," she replied. "I'm just being paranoid, I'll go by myself."

A week earlier, my mom had a small lump removed from the back of her arm. The doctor said it was probably nothing but he'd send the tissue to the lab for further testing. Dad was out of town when Mom got the call, so she naturally called me. I had almost forgotten that 3 P.M. phone call when the telephone it rang again at 5:30 P.M. just as we were sitting down for dinner.

Even though she didn't say a word, I could tell it was Mom on the other end. I had heard her cry before, but never like this. She was sobbing uncontrollably. It took me over three minutes just to get her calm enough to share the news. "Six weeks" were the first words out of her mouth. "The doctor said I have only six weeks to live…" "WHAT!" I shouted. "What kind of a nutcase are you seeing?"

For all intents and purposes, my mom looked healthy, but what they found was a metastasized malignant melanoma, the deadliest form of cancer. Melanoma lesions on the surface of the skin are easily treated; however, under the skin it is the deadliest. Quickly packing some clothes, we made the hour's drive to my parent's house.

We were the first to arrive, followed by Dr. Jon Paget, the family doctor. Jon was not the surgeon who gave Mom the bad news, but as soon as he got the report, he left the office, realizing the gravity of the situation. Don't let anyone tell you doctors don't make house calls! My dad arrived a few hours later, taking an emergency flight home from his meetings.

We all sat in the living room and cried, I mean cried our hearts out. We couldn't believe the news. My 60-year-old maternal grandmother had died of inoperable abdominal cancer within six months of the initial diagnosis. Now we were living it all over again, only at lightning speed. Jon told my parents he would work all night researching the disease and also attempt try to get Mom admitted to the University of Michigan Hospital which had the top melanoma clinic in the world.

Mom was examined at the U of M the next day and the doctors bluntly confirmed the diagnosis and the grim prognosis, stating there was nothing they could do for her and that, yes, according to the tests she would be dead in six weeks. They wanted her to return to the clinic so they could monitor her progress until her death. How grotesque!

Then they began to run tests on my mom. After the first week of tests, they bumped her diagnosis from six weeks to six months. Okay, some good news. The second week they gave her eighteen months to two years. Each week the diagnosis would improve. Six weeks to the day after explaining to her the prognosis, the doctors at the U of M declared my mother cancer free! As of the writing of this book it's now been six years!

I tell that story because in the midst of all our tears, my mom left us a legacy I will never forget. In the middle of that first night in her living room, with Dad, me, Laura, Dr. Jon and Mom all sobbing, suddenly Mom stops. She not only stopped crying, she began to laugh. Not just a chuckle or a snicker, but an all-out, no-holds barred guffaw! She could hardly contain herself. Mom would point at someone, and just bust a gut. When we finally got her calmed down, she said, "You know, in six weeks, I could be dead…gone…pushing up daisies. But if that is the case, then I just have one thing to say to each and every one of you…'It sucks to be you!' "

Now please don't be offended. My mom is one of the truest followers of Christ I know. She was simply stating both her legacy and the truth! If she died, she knew she'd be with Jesus, and in a whole lot better condition than any of us. Her legacy was simple: Follow Jesus.

You can leave a legacy that points people to Jesus by forming these daily habits.

Be Punctual

I am the son of a minister who was in the military. Therefore I do nothing in this world without guilt or fear! Growing up I remember hearing my father repeat these words time and time again: "Jay, if you're five minutes early, you're on time. If you're on time, you're late, and if you're late, you're rude!" I didn't quite know what to think of that statement, so I watched my dad to see if he lived the words he had spoken…and he did.

When I was 17, I asked my dad why he always made that statement. He told me: "Son, you will be late from time to time, like when the phone rings or there's heavy traffic or some other emergency. But, if you live your life always running late and always making others wait for you, you are telling the rest of the world that your time is more valuable than theirs, and Son, that is just plain rude."

If you want to leave a legacy that points people to Christ, start with treating all the people in your world with respect. One way to show that respect is to consider others time as valuable as your own. Make your marriage a union that honors each other by helping each other be punctual. If you tend to perpetually run late, then ask your spouse to help you manage your time better.

Be Polite

Occasionally, I'm invited to speak at a Youth for Christ camp in Florida. Three weeks in Florida at Spring Break hangin' out with teens on the beach. Rough assignment! Paul Miserlian directed the camp known as Florida Breakaway where YFC chapters from the Midwest had been bringing kids to Florida since the seventies. Paul (then the director in Findlay, Ohio) was a veteran who could take a couple weeks away and focus on the camp.

When not with the teens, Paul and I would hang out. One night in the dining room dinner included chicken and mashed potatoes, our third round of chicken and mashed potatoes in three weeks! I asked Paul, "Pass the salt and pepper." Paul just looked at me. So I repeated myself, a little louder; "Paul, the salt and pepper!" Again, Paul just looked at me.

Paul is a very sharp man. His silver hair and fit frame, coupled with a golden tan, didn't reveal his 60-plus years, but I knew how old he was and thought maybe he couldn't hear, so I almost yelled, "Paul, PASS THE SALT AND PEPPER!"

"Jay," he replied, "you know how much I care for you and appreciate what you're doing here with the teens. I have to tell you though that you are one of the most inconsiderate men I've ever met. In the two and a half weeks we've been together, not once have I heard you say the words 'please' or 'thank you.' What's worse, you didn't even change when your mom and dad were here. What gives?"

Whoosh, his words cut right to my heart, I'd never intended to be so inconsiderate, but Paul was right and I had no defense. I wish I could say that I've used the words "please" and "thank you" every day since. I haven't, but I try, and the variety of the responses I receive are amazing.

I was flying through Chicago O'Hare and, on a layover, entered one of those concession stands where you can get a hot dog and a

Coke for $18.00 (small exaggeration!). Standing in line behind a flight attendant, we both filled our Coke cups. She reached for a lid, and two stuck together. Instinctively, she separated them and handed one to me. I looked her in the eye and simply said, "Thank you." She whipped around and gave me a look like I'd just propositioned her. Stunned, I said "Hey, I'm sorry, I didn't mean anything." She just stood there and shook her head like she was trying to erase a memory.

"No, I'm sorry." She hesitated, then said, "I just got off a plane with 182 passengers, not one of them said thank you!" We live in an incredibly rude society. One of the best ways we can leave a legacy, pointing people to Christ, is to stand out as unique and different by challenging each other to practice simple politeness.

Be Practical

Laura enjoys watching the shows on HGTV where the host can make a magnificent holiday centerpiece out of two pinecones and some twine. Amazingly, nothing is wasted. As soon as a scrap of cloth is cut and falls, I ask myself, "How will they use that?" Thirty seconds later that same piece of cloth is plucked from obscurity and glued on a macramé box for the "finishing touch!" Argggh!

It drives me crazy because I'm a waster. Every trash day I lament how much our family throws out. I promise to do better and will do well for a while, and then boom! I open the refrigerator to find 18 colorful Tupperware bowls filled with moss green food in various stages of discomposure. My stomach turns and I don't know if it's from the smell or from the realization that our fridge is just a small reflection of a larger, more disturbing, issue—stewardship.

Jesus spoke more about money than almost any other issue. "For where your treasure is, there your heart will be also" (Matthew 6:21 NIV). His words cut to the quick when we realize how much we've been given, compared to how we often misuse it. Two godly financial advisors, Ron Blue and Larry Burkett, have helped countless couples in the constant battle they face to be good stewards of all God has given. Stand out, be different, be practical as a good steward, and leave a legacy that will point others to Christ.

Be Purposeful

Being a parent is tough. Little eyes and ears watch and hear everything you say. If you want to leave a legacy, you'd best be purposeful and do what you say!

Growing up in Northern Michigan, I learned to snow ski at an early age. Snow skiing is a sport custom-made for short people with thick legs, so I was a natural! Soon after we were married, I told Laura we were going to be a skiing family, and though snow in Atlanta is a rarity, her athletic ability made her a quick study. At three, Torrey joined us on the slopes.

For the next few years the snowfall varied; however, the year Torrey was nine, the snow was abundant and we returned to our favorite winter activity. The skiing was great, and Torrey took to the hills like a veteran. Late that afternoon as we rode up the chair lift Torrey said, "Dad, I'm glad you finally kept your word." "What!" I exclaimed. "What do you mean, kept my word?" "Well Dad, I remember you saying that we would always be a skiing family, and for the last three years we haven't skied. Now we are, I'm glad you kept your word."

Wow, from the mouths of babes. For all those years he'd remembered. All too often we do not realize the impact of what we say and how much others, particularly loved ones, cling to the thoughts we verbalize. As a result, we must be purposeful in all that we do.

If we are to leave a legacy that points other people to Jesus, we must live a purposeful life. Proverbs 3:5-6 encourages us to "Trust in the LORD with all your heart and lean not on your own understanding; in all your ways acknowledge him, and he will make your paths straight" (NIV). Walk the path of trust together.

Why not . . .

+ Discuss your views on time and how you use it.
+ Look for ways to be more practical around the house.
+ Strive for purpose in all you do.

Twelve

You Gotta
Like

*H*ave you ever thought about the ridiculous aspects of your life? I don't mean taxes and such, I'm talking about the everyday tasks that you do. What things are absurd? For me it is going grocery shopping! With some thought, I am sure you will agree.

Arriving at your local grocery store, you park the car, grab a grocery cart, and begin your journey through the barrage of advertisements calling out your name. Up and down each aisle. Proceeding to the the produce aisle, you examine a green pepper and put it in your cart. Rounding the corner to the bread aisle, you review the label to be sure it's the wheat bread that doesn't taste like cardboard and put it in your cart. You proceed down the cookie and canned veggie aisle, select a bag of double stuff Oreos and canned green beans. This process is repeated throughout the entire store...picking up food items and putting them into your cart.

Finally your cart is filled to the rim and you proceed to the checkout. What do you do there? You take each item that you have removed from the shelves out of your cart and place them on the conveyor belt. The cashier scans them and forwards the items to the bag person. Now it is the bag person's turn. What does he or she do? The bagger takes each item that you have removed from the shelves, placed in the cart, removed from the cart and placed on the conveyor belt, and puts them back into your cart! Again, the cart is full. Returning to your car, you take those food items that you have taken off the shelves and put into your cart, and taken out of the cart and put on the conveyor belt, and the bagger has taken off the conveyor belt and put back into your cart, and put them into your car. AHHHH! Now you can go home.

You arrive home. What do you do? All those groceries that you took off the shelves and put into your cart, and took out of your cart and put on the conveyor belt, and the bagger took off the conveyor belt and put into your cart, and you took out of the cart and put into your car...you now take out of your car and take them into your house. Once the groceries are all in your house, what do you do? YOU PUT THEM BACK ON SHELVES, which is where they started the day! Wouldn't it make more sense to just eat every meal out?

For some of you the answer to the question of what is ridiculous in your life may have been your spouse. At times, I am sure all of our spouses do things that seem ridiculous. That's when finding the humor in the situation can prove to be an asset.

Think back to what it was that first attracted you to your spouse. You may have met participating in a sport, hobby, or class. You may have met on a blind date. Whatever the scenario, marriage resulted because you enjoyed being with each other. You liked each other and you became and remain friends.

In order to celebrate your marriage, you gotta like. Now I know that some of you reading this right now are saying, "Like? Friends? You gotta be kidding. We hardly even cross paths anymore, what with our jobs, our children, our hobbies; our committee involvements. How are we supposed to be friends?"

By having fun together!

Find Commonalities

First you must find commonalities, things in which you share an interest. Think back to when you were first dating. What were the things you enjoyed doing together? Why not experience them again?!

Jay and I are blessed as we both are people who enjoy being active. We both like to exercise—I prefer aerobics and he likes to run—and we both enjoy sports. We often run together, watch televised sports events, and I'm working on my handicap in golf. Jay is attracted to individual sports and I would rather participate in team sports. We had to learn to give and take.

As children come along, or your children grow up and leave the nest, you will find your perspective on life changing. In growing older together, you may develop new hobbies, but make sure you include a common area of interest.

I cannot think of a better illustration than the process of Laura developing an appreciation for golf, my hobby of passion, although, it didn't start out so smooth. In Alma, Michigan, we have no less than 15 golf courses within a 30 minute drive. Folks in this locale spend their free time in the summer chasing the little white ball. Seeking to develop a working relationship with local business and church leaders, I would often find myself on one of the local courses. And my love of the game began to take root.

Laura never had much time for golf. "Stupid game!" she would remark as I watched the Masters Tournament being televised at beautiful Augusta National on Sunday afternoon. Laura is very social, so her passion was any sport that involved a team. Slowly but surely, she would find the time to play a round with me under the guise of a fun summertime "date." The occasional good hole or excellent shot proved to be just the "come backer" (a term used by golfers referring to a hole or shot played so well it made you want to come back for more!) she needed.

There is no substitute for good timing, and it all came together when Laura's friend Beth asked if she wanted to attend golf school. Three days away with her friends was incentive enough for Laura, plus it gave her the chance to hone her skills. Her love of the game was enough incentive for me to shell out the bucks, so off went my little weekend hacker.

Back came my dream girl! The love of my life now shares my most passionate hobby. Now instead of me begging for "golf dates," I am given the day and tee time to enter into my schedule. I am told which day in the next week will be our golf date. Now instead of dreaming of a golf vacation, Laura has developed specifications for the accommodations which include a view of the greens.

It is a tribute to her flexibility and willingness to learn that has given us golf as a common interest. Now she says all I have to do is learn to love to shop! ARRGH!!!

Uninterrupted Time Together

Second, we recommend you make finding uninterrupted time together a priority. Find creative ways to date. Go for walks, a bike ride, golf. Explore the course offerings in your local community as most colleges or universities offer six-week adult classes ranging from ballroom dancing to financial planning. Take a class together. Or you might choose to read a book together and then go out for dinner and discuss it. Whatever the activity, it is important that the time be uninterrupted. Over the years, we discovered two books we'd like to recommend on creative dating: *Creative Dating and More Creative Dating* by Doug Fields, and *10 Great Dates for Married Couples* by David and Claudia Arp.

If you're less than comfortable being alone for one reason or another, then group date. This was probably how you started dating members of the opposite sex when you were younger, and is a great way to begin the "dating" process all over again. Spending an evening with friends gives a couple an opportunity to laugh, share, and discuss adult issues with other adults. Often, the time spent in the car traveling home from a party or evening out can provide moments of intimacy which serve as building blocks for future encounters. Remember, too, you're never too old to enjoy a touch of adventure and smooch a little in the car!

If child care is a concern, it is money well spent to hire a baby sitter and invest time in your relationship. There are two reasons for this: 1) Children need to observe healthy male/female relationships. If Mom and Dad don't go out on dates, what motivation will they have to develop a healthy dating relationship of their own? If all the kids see are Mom and Dad flopped on the couch each night or, just as bad, working till all hours, where will they gain an appreciation for healthy interaction with other human beings? 2) All too soon our children will be graduating from high school or college and move out of the house to begin their own lives. Maintaining a close friendship with our spouse during the child-rearing years will build a strong relationship and prepare us for the "empty nest" years ahead.

One Thursday evening, Jay and I found ourselves at home without kids for the entire night. We were not sure how to spend our time, but finally decided to go for a run. After eating dinner, we indulged ourselves in adult conversation and enjoyed one of our favorite videos. We began to realize that we were experiencing a taste of our lifestyle in the year 2015 when Gracie enters college and we celebrated! Now don't get me wrong, we love our children dearly, but we look forward to the day when they will be on their own and we will have time together.

Never Quit Growing

Third, never quit growing. Life is cumulative. There is something new to learn every day. If we stop learning, we stop growing, and then we die. Jay is learning something new about me every day!

Read the newspaper. Invite a friend to join you for lunch. Learn a new hobby. I am learning to grow flowers in our yard. After purchasing a promising yellow rosebush, I soon found myself exploring the Internet to learn the latest technique to promote successful growth. Though I followed the instructions to the letter, it collapsed before my eyes! I discovered that starting with a rosebush to learn to grow flowers was not the best idea!

Installing a bird feeder in our backyard has provided an opportunity for Torrey, Grace, and me to learn about the birds that migrate in our locale. Everyday we look forward to watching the various species munch on the seeds we've provided. We have discovered that if we put different bird seed in the feeder, different types of birds are attracted to dine at our table.

There is so much uncharted territory in our world, our lives, and our spouse's lives that await discovery! Life is an adventure...we can never stop growing! The truth is we need each other's feedback to grow!

What kind of tree are you?

The trouble with most of us is that we have grown up in a country that prides itself on rugged individualism where "pull yourself up by your bootstraps" or "I did it my way" are common themes. We see ourselves like the great white pine tree.

The magnificent white pine grows to heights of nearly 150 feet and has a tap root that grows as deep into the Michigan sand as the tree stands high. We see ourselves as having deep roots that allow us to firmly "stand alone" against all odds, though we are very different. In truth, we are very different. In fact, the Bible frequently describes how much we depend on each other and we should not try to stand alone. "Though one may be overpowered, two can defend themselves. A cord of three strands is not quickly broken" (Ecclesiastes 4:12 NIV).

The pride of northern California is the amazing giant sequoia tree which reaches a height of over 300 feet. The tree's circumference surpasses the arm spread of four to five adults attempting to encircle its girth. For its massive size the sequoia has an incredibly shallow root system as the roots of this mighty tree reach a depth of only five or six feet.

How then does this tree stand secure against the fierce Pacific storms and winds? Simple. You will never see a sequoia stand alone. Sequoias grow in and around and only survive among, other sequoia trees. While their roots grow only to a shallow depth, they diverge in every direction for nearly 150 feet. Their roots become intertwined with other sequoias and gain tremendous strength.

What a perfect picture of how we should grow together as a couple. The very first blessing God ever gave was when He blessed Adam with Eve and vice versa. You have been given a blessing in your spouse and as you reach out and grow toward each other, your root systems will intertwine and gain strength from one another. If you are a Christian, then you are probably familiar with Paul's teaching on the body; how each one of us needs to rely and depend on the other. Marriage is the perfect place to practice that reliance—by growing together as a couple and living in the fulfillment that gives you a reason to celebrate.

Why not...

+ Make a list of all the things you and your spouse can do together.
+ Decide to make uninterrupted time every day, even if its just five minutes.
+ Look for new opportunities to grow together.

CeleBRATe
your marriage!

Bring a Celebrate Your Marriage
Workshop to Your Home Church!

Jay and Laura Laffoon have a unique way of bringing joy and celebration to the lives of married couples in your church. Celebrate your marriage workshops can be custom-designed to meet the unique needs of your congregation!

"Jay and Laura connect—especially as a team. Their unique communication styles balance the presentation with humor, real-life, tremendous insight, and fun application. We will have them back again!"

Joel Herron
Fountain City Wesleyan Church
Richmond, Indiana

Contact us!
http://celebrateyourmarriage.com

CELEBRATE!
P.O. Box 93
Alma, MI 48801

Booking information:
Contact: Danny deArmas
(407)282-9098
dannyde@celebrateministries.com

AlSO...

Experience Celebrate Your Marriage Conferences

CELEBRATE YOUR MARRIAGE
OPRYLAND HOTEL
Nashville, TN

Step into Opryland Hotel Nashville and enter a whole new world, a place where you'll experience all the charm and elegance of the South. Explore nine acres of lush indoor gardens, winding pathways, and sparkling waterfalls.

CELEBRATE YOUR MARRIAGE
GRAND HOTEL
Mackinac Island, MI

Grand Hotel beckons you to a bygone era of old-world hospitality and charm.

Check for dates online today!
http://celebrateyourmarriage.com
Or call 989.466.5574

About the Authors

Jay and Laura Laffoon

*J*ay and Laura Laffoon are a dynamic and inspirational couple who help others CELEBRATE their marriage! Building marriages by offering unique opportunities for celebration, Jay and Laura focus couples on basic principles often lost in the day-to-day hustle and bustle.

The Laffoon's unique and motivating seminars have been shared throughout the United States and Canada. Jay and Laura annually host over 1,000 couples at beautiful Grand Hotel on Mackinac Island, Michigan. Their presentations are full of humor, real life experiences, and Biblical truth. Couples walk away challenged and enriched.

Make Love Everyday
Order Form

Postal orders: P.O. Box 93
Alma, MI 48801

Telephone orders: 989-466-5574

E-mail orders: info@celebrateministries.com

Please send *Make Love Everyday* to:

Name: _____

Address: _____

City: _____ State: _____

Zip: _____

Telephone: (_____) _____

Book Price: $12.00

Shipping: $3.00 for the first book and $1.00 for each additional book to cover shipping and handling within US, Canada, and Mexico. International orders add $6.00 for the first book and $2.00 for each additional book.

Or order from:
ACW Press
5501 N. 7th. Ave. #502
Phoenix, AZ 85013

(800) 931-BOOK

or contact your local bookstore